A Short History of
Brazil

D0745734

www.pocketessentials.com

Other Pocket Essentials by Gordon Kerr

A Short History of Europe
A Short History of Africa
A Short History of China
A Short History of The First World War

A
Short History
of Brazil

GORDON KERR

POCKET ESSENTIALS

First published in 2014 by Pocket Essentials,
an imprint of Oldcastle Books Ltd,
P.O.Box 394, Harpenden, Herts,
AL5 1XJ, UK
www.pocketessentials.com

Editor: Nick Rennison

A CIP catalogue record for this book is available from the British Library.

ISBN
978-1-84344-196-0 (Print)
978-1-84344-197-7 (epub)
978-1-84344-198-4 (kindle)
978-1-84344-199-1 (pdf)

2 4 6 8 10 9 7 5 3 1

Typeset by Avocet Typeset, Somerton, Somerset
in 9.75pt Univers Light
Printed and bound in Great Britain by CPI Group (Ltd), Croydon, CR0 4YY

For Diane, as always

Acknowledgements

I would like to express my thanks to Ion Mills for commissioning a series of books that are a joy to research and write; Claire Watts for her hard work and undivided attention; and my editor Nick Rennison, for his encouragement and irritatingly single-minded devotion to detail, as well as for his many years of friendship. Also, thanks to Dr David Dent for the benefit of his Brazilian knowledge.

Contents

Introduction

Our knowledge of Brazil is surprisingly limited, considering the vast size of the country. What do we know of it, after all? There is Carnival, of course: gaudy costumes, vibrant samba, an outpouring of hedonistic exhibitionism that colours most people's view of the country. There is also football: the Brazilian team of Pele and Jairzinho in the 1970 World Cup, playing with smiles on their faces, bringing the exuberance of carnival to the football pitch with what cliché-bound commentators often described as 'silky' skills. We are also likely to know about the Amazon, the immense waterway at which we have all marvelled on television wildlife programmes, a region that is home to an astonishingly diverse range of flora, fauna and wildlife.

What most people are sadly ignorant of, however, is the fascinating history of this vast land, how it came into being, its struggles with Portugal as well as with itself over the five centuries of its existence as a nation, how it has striven to remain unified and to govern itself in the face of the huge difficulties presented by distance, greed and ambition.

The story of Brazil is a complex one involving the extraordinary relocation of an entire royal court; a military that on numerous occasions was not prepared to stand on the sidelines; the suicide of a dictator beloved of many of his people; a dark period of torture, imprisonment and death when the country was treated as a pariah by most of the international community; and an astonishing economic flowering that has given Brazil one of the world's leading economies.

History is the story of people, often extraordinary people, and Brazil has had its share of those. The stories of its first emperors read like soap operas, with mistresses, difficult marriages, abandonment by parents and hearts torn by decisions about the best way for their country to be governed. Brazilian history is also littered with dramatic moments such as *Dia de Fico* (I Shall Stay Day), when Prince Pedro, later Emperor Pedro I, announced that he would remain in Brazil instead of obeying the demand of the Portuguese parliament that he return to Portugal. Or there is the moment when Getúlio Vargas, who had governed Brazil for eighteen years in two different periods, mostly in a dictatorial manner, put a gun to his heart and pulled the trigger rather than face the ignominy of being ousted from power for a second time. Moments such as these herald a change in a nation's fortunes, a move in a new direction, shaping the lives of millions alive then and those of generations to come.

Brazil has had its share of dark moments, of course, none darker than the twenty-one years of military rule its people endured from 1964 to 1985. A succession of generals was selected to rule the country, taking it in a downward spiral into terrible violence and fierce repression. Politicians, artists, musicians and writers whose very lives were in danger, fled the country and fought their repressors from exile. Many who could not, or who chose to stay and fight on their own soil, either faced long periods of incarceration and torture or simply disappeared at the hands of the death squads that roamed the streets of Brazil's cities, killing on behalf of the generals.

Just twenty-nine years later, Brazil is a different country, a vibrant, multicultural nation whose economy is the envy of the world. There remain grave problems, of course, of inequality, poverty, poor social welfare provision and pollution. Brazil's future success in dealing with these issues will determine its place in the world in years to come.

But, for now, it is a country that is going places, a country whose time has come and a country about which we should all know a little more.

1

The Geography of Brazil

Brazil is a vast country, the fifth largest in the world after Russia, Canada, China and the United States. With a total area of 3,287,612 square miles, it also has the world's fifth largest population – estimated in 2013 to be 201,032,714. It is the biggest country in South America, occupying 47 per cent of the continent. Its Atlantic coastline stretches for 4,655 miles and it shares almost 10,000 miles of inland borders with a number of other South American nations – Uruguay to the south; Argentina, Paraguay and Bolivia to the southwest; Peru to the west; Colombia to the northwest; and to the north, Venezuela, Guyana, Suriname and French Guiana. In fact, it shares a border with every South American country except Ecuador and Chile.

From the Amazon basin in the north and west to the Highlands of the southeast of the country, Brazil enjoys a diverse topography that includes hills, mountains, plains, highlands and scrublands. Its most important geographical feature is the Amazon River. The second-longest river in the world, it flows for approximately 4,300 miles before draining into the Atlantic Ocean. In terms of water-flow it is by far the largest river in the world, accounting for around a fifth of the world's total river-flow and it plays host to the world's most extensive virgin rainforest. Its great tributaries include the Juruá, Purus, Madeira, Tapajós, and Xingu rivers on the southern side and the Rio Negro to the north. In places, it is impossible to see from one side to the other and a large part of it boasts a depth of one hundred feet. In fact, small ocean-going vessels are able to navigate all the way from the Atlantic to Iquitos in Peru, a distance of 2,300 miles. The Amazon and its tributaries were vital in enabling the exploration of the north and west of Brazil and the Amazon Basin enjoys unparalleled biodiversity, with more than a third of all the world's species inhabiting its rainforest.

The country's highest point is Pico da Neblina, which reaches 9,888 feet, but the Brazilian Highlands and plateaus generally average less than 4,000 feet in height. The terrain is more rugged in the southeast where extensive uplands fall away quickly at the Atlantic coast, much of which is composed of the wall-like geographical feature known as the Great Escarpment that separates the highland plateau from the shoreline. Behind it lie mountain ranges such as the Mantiqueira and the Serra do Mar. The northwestern part of the plateau is made up of rolling terrain interrupted by low, rounded hills. In the north of the country, the Guiana Highlands form a wedge between rivers flowing southwards into the Amazon Basin and rivers that drain into the Orinoco River system in Venezuela, beyond Brazil's northern border.

Brazil is home to five major types of climate – equatorial, tropical, semi-arid, highland tropical, and subtropical – which provide the country with a variety of environments. In the north there are equatorial forests and the northeast boasts semi-arid desert conditions. Temperate coniferous forests flourish in the south and in the centre of the country can be found tropical savannas. Microclimates abound. The semi-arid region in the northeast receives less than 31.5 inches of rain per year and occasionally less than that, leading to prolonged periods of drought. In central Brazil, the rainfall is more seasonal, as could be expected of a savanna climate. In the south, near the coast, rain falls throughout the year and the area generally enjoys temperate conditions with cool winters and even frosts and snowfall on higher ground.

Modern Brazil is divided into 26 states and a Federal District but the Instituto Brasileiro de Geografia e Estatística has divided the country into five main geographic divisions. The North consists of the southern slopes of the Guiana Highland and the northern Brazilian Highlands as well as the Amazon Basin. The Northeast, recognised as the birthplace of Brazil, is renowned for its hot climate, stunning beaches and rich cultural tradition, including Carnival. Of its 53.6 million inhabitants, about 15 million live on the arid hinterland or *sertão*, while the rest live in urban centres such as Salvador, Recife and Fortaleza. The Centre-West region is home to Brazil's purpose-built capital, Brasília, in the area known as *Distrito Federal* (Federal District). Other areas are the flat Mato Grosso and Mato Grosso do Sul consisting of much of the Pantanal, one of the world's largest tropical wetland areas. The Southeast region of Brazil is the country's wealthiest area, representing around 60 per cent of its GDP. It contains São Paolo, Rio de Janeiro and Minas Gerais, the country's richest states.

2

Pre-Colonial Peoples

Prehistory to 1500

Many histories of Brazil begin their narrative on Wednesday 22 April 1500, the day on which Portuguese explorer, Pedro Álvares Cabral (c1467–c1520), anchored his ship near Monte Pascoal in what is currently the state of Bahia in northeastern Brazil. The Portuguese were not the first people to set foot on this land, of course. Before their arrival, there are estimated to have been between 2 and 4 million indigenous people, living in some 2,000 nations and tribes in Brazil's rich coastal zone, from the modern-day states of Maranhão and Pará in the North to Santa Catarina in the South.

The origins of the native peoples of South America are the subject of debate amongst archaeologists. One theory holds that they arrived between 13,000 and 17,000 years ago, migrating from North Asia across the Bering Land Bridge that connected Asia and North America at various times during the Ice Age. This view is challenged, however, by the discovery of human remains in South America that appear to date from up to 20,000 years ago. Recent finds appear to be morphologically different to the Asian type and, in fact, these remains are closer to Australian Aborigines. This has given rise to a theory suggesting that these earlier immigrants might have voyaged across the ocean on boats or sea-going rafts or could possibly have travelled north along the coast of Asia and into America over the Bering Strait. Many believe, however, that this journey would have been impossible. Even more difficult to believe is a theory that they made their way from Australia along the coast of Antarctica to the tip of South America.

On the eve of the arrival of the Portuguese there were several groupings of Brazilian natives, the main ones being the Mundurukú, the Tupinambá and the Yanomami.

On the coast, the Tupinambá were the main group, speaking 'Tupi', which is part of the Tupi-Guarani language family comprising more than 40 language groups that are in evidence throughout Latin America. Twenty-one Tupi-Guarani languages are spoken in Brazil, mostly in the areas of the modern states of Maranhão and Pará in the North and Mato Grasso in the Centre-West. The fact that Tupi-Guarani speakers exist in Bolivia, Peru, Argentina, French Guiana, Venezuela and Colombia demonstrates the extent to which these peoples migrated in the centuries before European colonisation. They may have migrated in search of new sources of food or they may have been forced to move by war. They may have journeyed for religious reasons but it may simply have been climate change that persuaded them to go off in search of new territories.

The Tupinambá had emigrated from the south centuries prior to the arrival of the Europeans and lived on the coast from Ceará in the north to Porto Alegre in the south, in villages that were home to between 400 and 1,600 inhabitants organised by family. They occupied large dwellings more than 500 feet long and 100 feet wide, the male leader of the community occupying the area at the head of the house with his wives and servants. The Tupinambá hunted for food and augmented their diet of fish and game with crops cultivated on land adjacent to their village. For the Tupinambá, warfare was constant, their religious and social values delineated by it. Ritual cannibalism formed part of their ceremonial activities. The survival of a generation was guaranteed, they believed, by the consumption of human flesh that would placate the spirits and allow them to gain the wisdom of their ancestors. The Tupinambá resisted the Portuguese and

French settlers, joining together in confederations to fight efforts to enslave them or corral them in Jesuit missions. They fled the coast, scattering into the distant interior, but disease and further Portuguese incursions – especially the war waged against them by the Portuguese Governor General of Brazil, Mem de Sá (c1500–72), between 1557 and 1572 – greatly reduced their number.

The Mundurukú migrated to the area of modern Mato Grosso around 1000 AD and began to live in forests and engage in agricultural pursuits. The leader, or headman, of a settlement had both political and religious duties, responsible for maintaining the myths of his community and acting as a channel for spiritual messages to his people from the gods. Like the Tupinambá, warfare played a large part in the lives of the Mundurukú and they travelled far and wide on land and on rivers to secure sacrificial heads, believing that only when another group was subdued by force and ritually sacrificed would balance be achieved in the universe. They were skilled with the bow and arrow and their society was male-dominated, women barred from male-only huts where the men swapped tales of hunting prowess. The men hunted jaguars, deer, monkeys, tapirs and birds while the women of the village trapped smaller game. Their diet was augmented by manioc – also known as cassava – and they lived in thatched dwellings on poles situated on grassy hills from which they could survey their territory.

When the Europeans arrived, the Yanomami lived in isolated villages and practised communal agriculture, growing plantains, cassava, tubers, corn and other vegetables which were supplemented by fruits, nuts, seeds, grubs and honey. They hunted a variety of wildlife. Yanomami culture valued aggressive behaviour and American anthropologist, Napoleon Chagnon, has described them as living in 'a state of chronic warfare'.

During the years since that first Portuguese ship dropped anchor, the number of indigenous people in Brazil has drastically declined, a decline hastened by slavery, captivity in Catholic missions and the European lust for gold and land. Mostly, however, they have been decimated by diseases brought by the Europeans. By the end of Brazil's colonial period, slaves who had been transported from their African homelands made up 38 per cent of the population of Brazil; whites, mixed race people and freed blacks represented 56 per cent; but the indigenous peoples who had lived and hunted on these lands for centuries amounted to only 6 per cent.

Today, there are 818,000 indigenous people in more than 220 tribes scattered across the country. Their individual cultures are fading; 110 of the tribal languages of Brazil are spoken by fewer than 400 people and some tribes, such as the Akuntsu and the Kanoê number little more than a few dozen members.

3

Colonial Brazil
1500 to 1822

The Age of Discovery

In 1453, the Ottoman Empire's conquest of Constantinople, coupled with the Italian Maritime Republics' control of the Mediterranean, brought an end to Europe's lucrative overland trade with Asia, persuading many to seek routes to the east by sea. This heralded the start of what has become known as the Age of Discovery, or Age of Exploration, the period between the fifteenth and seventeenth centuries during which Europeans explored Africa, the Americas, Asia and Oceania, initially trying to discover a route to the 'East Indies' by which the money-spinning trade in gold, silver and spices could continue, but establishing new colonies in the process.

Initially, Spain and Portugal were the two principals in this perilous expansion of the known world. In fact, Portugal began its exploration some hundred years before the Genoese sailor, Christopher Columbus (1451–1506), made his historic journey to the Americas, sailing under the Spanish flag. The Portuguese had already gained a great deal of experience in long-distance trade and their proximity to the islands of the Atlantic and the coast of Africa encouraged maritime travel. The currents on which sea-going vessels relied were particularly favourable to the ports of Portugal and southwest Spain and added to this was the fact that Portugal was a stable, unified kingdom, facing no external threat at a time when France, England, Spain and Italy were mired in wars and internal strife. This relative peace had transpired following the revolution of 1383–85, a peasant revolt similar to the ones that broke out elsewhere in Europe at the time. In the Portuguese case, however, it ended very differently, after the king of Castile in modern northern Spain, invaded the country, supported by the Portuguese aristocracy. Thus did the struggle become one of national independence and ended with the revolution's central protagonist, Prince João (r. 1385–1433), illegitimate son of Pedro I (1357–67) of Portugal, on the throne. Power was consolidated in João, enabling Portugal to contemplate the great ventures of the next few decades in comparative peace.

Each section of Portuguese society had reason to embrace overseas expansion with enthusiasm. The king saw it as a way to increase revenue flooding into the royal coffers; the Church relished the thought of new Christian converts; for the merchants, of course, there was the tantalising prospect of new markets and new products; and even the ordinary citizen perceived opportunity in these new lands, the chance to make a new and better life in exotic climes. The time was right. New maritime technology had been introduced that facilitated the extensive voyages that had to be endured. Navigators were able to use improved quadrants and astrolabes to plot their course by the stars. The Portuguese had invented the caravel, a light fast vessel whose shallow draft allowed it to sail close to land. Used extensively in the navigation of the coastlines of Africa and Brazil, it enabled Portugal to become Europe's pre-eminent sea power during the fifteenth century.

In 1492, when Columbus reached America, arriving at the Antilles, Portugal disputed Spanish ownership of the new land. This led to a series of negotiations that produced the 1494 Treaty of Tordesillas, an agreement between the two superpowers that effectively divided the world into two hemispheres. Land discovered west of a line 370 leagues west of the Cape Verde Islands would belong to Spain; that discovered east of the line would be assigned to Portugal.

The principal objective of these maritime ventures was to find gold and spices. Gold, it goes without saying, was vital as a reliable means of exchange and was also used to decorate clothing and the bodies of Portuguese aristocrats. Methods of preserving meat were, at the time, fairly primitive and spices helped to disguise the taste of rotting flesh. Eventually, after 1441, the Portuguese began to specialise in human cargo, heralding the beginning of the slave trade that would continue for more than three centuries.

The first man to realise the commercial opportunities offered by the world's oceans was the Portuguese Prince Henry (1394–1460), also known as Henry 'the Navigator'. From his residence in Vila do Infante on the Sagres Peninsula, at the most southwestern point of Iberia, with access to both the Atlantic and Mediterranean Oceans, Henry sponsored voyages of exploration down the west coast of Africa. Reaching as far south as Guinea, Portuguese ships brought back slaves and goods, establishing a series of fortified trading posts or *feitorias* at intervals along the coast. Eventually, in a voyage of 1497–99, Portuguese explorer, Vasco da Gama (c1460–1524), brought east and west together for the first time when he rounded the Cape of Good Hope and made his way up the East African coast and across the Indian Ocean to Calicut on the coast of southwest India.

Cabral and the Discovery of Brazil

Little is known about the life of Pedro Cabral prior to the voyage that resulted in the discovery of Brazil except that he was young – 32 or 33 years old – a minor noble, and may have campaigned in North Africa. On 15 February 1500, he was appointed commander of a fleet assembled to follow up on Vasco da Gama's expedition. It is possible that Cabral had little or no naval experience; it was the custom of the Portuguese king to appoint nobles to naval and military commands regardless of experience. Thus, on 8 March 1500, amidst great pageantry, with King Manuel I (r.1495–1521) present, thirteen ships carrying twelve hundred men set sail from the mouth of the Tagus River. They sailed into the far western Atlantic – perhaps intentionally – and fifty-three days later, on 20 April, the sighting of seaweed and birds signalled the approach of land. The following afternoon the fleet dropped anchor off the northeast coast of modern-day Brazil near Monte Pascoal (Easter Mount) about thirty-nine miles to the south of the modern-day city of Porto Seguro, in the state of Bahia.

On 23 April, Cabral sent ashore one of his captains, Nicolau Coelho (c1460–1502), who had sailed with da Gama. Coelho claimed the land for the Portuguese Crown as it lay east of the demarcation line set by the Treaty of Tordesillas. On the shore by this time had gathered a group of curious indigenous people with whom Coelho exchanged gifts. When the landing party returned to the ship, Cabral ordered the fleet northwards, anchoring the following day in a natural harbour that was named Porto Seguro (Safe Port). On 26 April, Cabral and his sailors participated in the first Mass on Brazilian soil beneath a huge wooden cross, some 23 feet long, which they had built. Believing this new land to be an island, Cabral named it Ilha de Vera Cruz (Island of the True Cross) and a ship was immediately dispatched back to Portugal to inform the king of his new possession. Cabral's fleet re-provisioned and turned east towards the Cape of Good Hope and India.

Colonisation

For some time, people shared Cabral's initial view that the land that would become Brazil was nothing more than a large island and, indeed, news of its discovery was greeted with none of the celebration generated by Vasco da Gama's voyage to India. In fact, no one seems to have considered that there was any potential in the land other than as a place inhabited by exotic birds and strange people. Some named it 'Land of the Parrots' while King Manuel I initially christened it Vera Cruz before changing it to Santa Cruz. Amerigo Vespucci (1454–1512), the Florentine navigator, joined the next expedition to the new land in 1501 with the objective of mapping the coastline. It was in a letter to his former employer Lorenzo di Pier Francesco de' Medici (1463–1503) that Vespucci coined the term 'New World' for the new territories. Brazil, meanwhile, continued to be known as Santa Cruz.

In 1502, the Portuguese government leased the new territory to a consortium of Lisbon merchants, led by Fernão de Loronha (c1470–c1540). They established a business on the coast harvesting brazilwood, a wood that produces a red dye much in demand by the European cloth industry that until then had to be imported at great expense from India. Between 1502 and 1510, while Loronha's consortium held the monopoly on brazilwood from the newly discovered land, the territory's name gradually began to reflect its principal resource, changing to *Terra do Brasil* (Land of Brazil), its inhabitants becoming known as *Brasileiros*. There were decent profits to be made from brazilwood, which resulted in merchants of other nations taking an interest. The French, who did not recognise the Treaty of Tordesillas, engaged in trade and piracy along a Brazilian coast far too long to be properly policed by the Portuguese. The French established settlements in Guanabara Bay (Rio de Janeiro) and in the modern state of Maranhão in the North.

In 1530, Portuguese King João III (r.1521–1527) remedied this situation by dispatching Martim Afonso de Sousa (c1500–1571) with an expedition designed to patrol the coast and establish a proper colony. In 1532, the colony of São Vicente was established, close to the present-day city of Santos. In distributing the land to colonists, Afonso created a template for the future of Brazilian land distribution, doling it out with lavish generosity. People were given large tracts to cultivate as sugar plantations and when land in the interior was later distributed, the resulting farms dwarfed even the massive coastal estates.

To manage this vast territory, the king introduced a system that harked back to feudal times in Europe, creating hereditary captaincies, by which fifteen large swathes of land were each awarded to a so-called donatory captain. The captains were made up of a variety of professions – merchants, bureaucrats and minor aristocrats – who were allowed to manage the land and collect fees and taxes from any enterprise on it although their endowment from the king did not make them owners. Instead, they received a percentage of tributes paid to the Crown. These approximations of feudal lords were given the right to administer justice as well as the power to found towns and conscript men for military duty. They also had the right to distribute individual plots of land – *samaras* – that resulted in the creation of huge *latifúndios* (estates). These tracts of virgin land had to be cultivated within five years or a financial penalty had to be paid to the Crown which retained a monopoly over the produce of this land. Needless to say, an array of officials had to be appointed in order to deal with the ensuing bureaucratic requirements.

Apart from those at São Vicente and Pernambuco, the captaincies soon fell victim to lack of experience in governance as well as lack of resources. They were not helped by the hostile environment in which the settlers lived, rendered even more difficult by attacks by the French and local tribes. Through time, therefore, the government bought them back and re-established control of them, the king deciding instead to appoint a governor-general to supervise his Brazilian colony. He chose for the role a loyal military man, Tomé de Sousa (1503–79), who, accompanied by a large number of soldiers as well as officials and craftsmen, arrived in the Baía de Todos os Santos in Bahia in March 1549. There they began constructing a capital, a fortified stronghold known as Salvador (da Bahia). Centralisation of the administration of the colony proved difficult, however, the extremes of weather and the vast distances that had to be covered rendering communication all but impossible. Throughout the sixteenth century, Portugal's new colony continued to underwhelm, delivering in 1588, for example, just 2.5 per cent of the Crown's revenues while the far more successful Portuguese India delivered 26 per cent.

It proved wise to send soldiers to Brazil to support the governor-general because both de Sousa and his successor, Mem de Sá, who occupied the governor-general role from 1558 to 1572, faced a threat from the French who were themselves making efforts to colonise Brazil. In 1555, with the help of the Tamoios, a Tupí tribe, they established a settlement named 'French Antarctica' in the area of modern-day Rio de Janeiro. The Portuguese reacted aggressively and the interlopers were eventually expelled in 1567. A new Portuguese settlement was established in Guanabara Bay and named (São Sebastião do) Rio de Janeiro but France's continued efforts to undermine Portuguese authority in Brazil forced the colonists to build fortified settlements along the Brazilian coastline. This brought them into contact as well as into conflict with the local indigenous people who were subdued and more often than not converted to Christianity. The half-dozen Jesuits, led by Father Manuel da Nóbrega (1517–1570), who had arrived with Tomé de Sousa in 1549, had been working ever since to pacify the native people.

Following a succession crisis, Portugal fell under Spanish rule between 1580 and 1640. In 1580, Philip II of Spain was crowned Philip I of Portugal and the Algarves (r. 1581–98), the first ruler of what has become known as the Iberian Union. It was a period during which Portugal was permitted to remain relatively autonomous and that certainly applied to their governorship of the colonies which remained under the control of officials in Lisbon. 1604 saw the creation of the *Conselho da India e Conquistas Ultramarinas* (Council for India and Overseas Conquests) to control the entire Portuguese Empire, including Brazil. But by this time Brazil was beginning to assume greater importance, as demonstrated by the judicial powers given to the *Tribunal da Relação* (High Court of Appeals), established in Bahia in 1609. In 1621 the colony was split into two in order to make it easier to govern. The *Estado do Brasil* (State of Brazil) contained all the territory settled during the sixteenth century, and was governed from Salvador while the State of Maranhão, with its capital located at São Luís, contained the captaincies of Grão-Pará, Maranhão and Ceará. In spite of this, however, any centralisation of government remained impracticable due to the great distances that separated settlements. As a result, local affairs remained decentralised during the entire colonial period with the population concentrated in numerous small municipalities, often located in the vicinity of large sugar plantations. The owners of those plantations – *homens bons* (leading citizens) – made up the town councils of the municipalities, which had far-reaching political, fiscal, judicial and even policing powers over the region. Often, if they judged them to be contrary to their own local interests, these councils overruled orders from the Crown.

War With the Dutch

From 1519, the Netherlands formed one of the Seventeen Provinces ruled by the Holy Roman Emperor and King of Spain, Charles V (r. 1519–56). In 1579 the northern half of the Seventeen Provinces, weary of Spanish rule, established the Union of Utrecht by which they swore to support each other against Philip II of Spain (r. 1554–98). In 1581, they formally deposed Philip and declared independence. Until then, the Dutch had provided ships, credit and markets for Brazilian goods but the Spanish now tried to end that participation in trade with the colony. The Dutch, on the other hand, eager to hit back at Spain by wresting Brazil from the Portuguese, invaded Bahia in 1623, only withdrawing a year later. In 1630, they attacked Pernambuco, capturing Recife and holding it for twenty years, during which time it grew from a small settlement to a large port. It was governed by the Dutch nobleman, Count Johan Maurits of Nassau (1604–79) on behalf of the Dutch East India Company and was named New Holland. During Maurits' tenure as governor, New Holland stretched from Pernambuco to the mouth of the Amazon. With the help of the Dutch architect Pieter Post (1608–69), he transformed Recife, re-naming it Mauritsstad and constructing splendid public buildings and beautiful gardens. The capture of Recife was a strategically sound move because not only was it the most profitable region in Brazil, it also provided the Dutch with a base from which to launch attacks on Portuguese feitorias in West Africa and Angola. It also gave them control of the increasingly lucrative transatlantic slave trade. They were now able to disrupt Portuguese and Spanish trade routes with the east and inhibit Spain's control of its South American colonies.

In Pernambuco, local plantation owners eventually had little option but to sign an agreement with the Dutch. However, when the count fell out with his masters at the Dutch East India Company and returned to Europe in 1644, renewed conflict broke out, with naval battles and a struggle on land known as the Pernambucan Insurrection. The local colonists were victorious, eventually expelling the Dutch in 1654. It was the last foreign invasion Brazil would experience.

In Europe, meanwhile, the Iberian Union had been ended by a 1640 revolution staged by Portuguese nobility and bourgeoisie while Spain was preoccupied by the Thirty Years' War and by another uprising in Catalonia. The Portuguese people proclaimed João IV (r.1640–56), of the House of Braganza, King of Portugal. Acknowledging the increasing importance of his Brazilian colony, João declared it a principality, the heir to the Crown from then on assuming the title 'Prince of Brazil'. Two years later, the *Conselho Ultramarino* (Overseas Council) was constituted in another effort to govern the distant and unwieldy colony.

The Church

Six Jesuits arrived with Tomé de Sousa in 1549, although from the time of Cabral, men of religion had travelled with every expedition. Before 1549, the Church had made relatively little impact on the new colony, more concerned with the spiritual needs of the colonists than the conversion of the local indigenous peoples. Between 1549 and 1598 only 128 Jesuits arrived in Brazil, but their work would leave a lasting impression on the country as they began to introduce religion to the indigenous peoples and, for the next two hundred years, provided education.

Brazil had initially been part of the diocese of Funchal in the Azores but in 1551 it became a bishopric. The bishop's residence was established in Salvador which was named as capital by the governor-general. In 1676, an archbishop was appointed and two new bishoprics were founded, at Rio de Janeiro and Pernambuco. By 1800, there were four more – Pará, Maranhão, São Paulo and Mariana in Minas Gerais. The African bishopric of São Tomé also fell under the control of the Archbishop of Bahia in Salvador. Jesuit priests who had learned African languages proved particularly useful in the conversion of African slaves who had made the crossing. The Franciscans, who had actually arrived in Brazil before the Jesuits, also played an important part in Christianising the country. Eventually, by the end of the sixteenth century, they had been joined by Capuchins, Benedictines and Carmelites. Voluntary groups, known as *irmandades*, built churches and maintained charitable institutions like hospitals and orphanages. Meanwhile, the Inquisition lingered in the background to deal with cases of corruption or backsliding, the latter often involving 'New Christians', as Jewish converts were called. The Inquisition visited the colony three times. Between 1591 and 1595, it held court in Salvador and Olinda; in 1681, it returned to Salvador; and between 1763 and 1769, it was active in Belém. On the whole, though, there seems to have been a greater degree of toleration in Brazil than in the rest of the Roman Catholic world.

The conversion of indigenous people to Christianity was taken in hand by the Jesuits, led by Manuel da Nóbrega and José de Anchieta (1534–97). They created a system which involved gathering the indigenous people into villages where they were taught Christian values. While some point to the fact that the Jesuits extracted a Papal bull stating that they were human and should be protected, others claim that these villages enabled the Jesuits to exploit the local people's potential for labour. They were taught trades and skills but were rigidly controlled by the few Jesuit priests who administered these missions. They became subjects of the king in Lisbon, wore European clothes and, most importantly for the Crown, contributed to the royal coffers.

Agriculture was encouraged by the governor-general, especially the production of sugar, an expensive luxury to Europeans at the time. The number of sugar mills increased but suffered from a shortage of labour. The Portuguese tried using native people, firstly as slaves, then as a type of indigenous peasantry and then as workers earning a wage. But none of these approaches was successful, the indigenous population proving totally unsuitable. Planters and Jesuits were at odds over the labour issue, the planters resenting the Jesuits' and, indeed, the Church's opposition to the native Brazilians being forced to work. Ultimately, none of this mattered because the indigenous peoples were unwilling to give up their lifestyles for work that brought them little or no benefit. Capitalism was anathema to them.

Nonetheless, the colonial pattern of Brazilian life was soon well established. The country was dominated socially and economically by large plantations and their owners; agriculture was there to produce goods for export to Europe; labour was to be exploited and subservience had to be shown.

Westward Expansion

One major benefit the Iberian Union brought was the removal of the restrictions placed upon Spain and Portugal by the 1494 Treaty of Tordesillas. This permitted the Portuguese to expand their territory in Brazil, exploring the interior in search of precious metals. There they also hoped to find indigenous people who could be enslaved to work on the rapidly growing sugar plantations. During the seventeenth century, numerous *bandeira* (flag) expeditions, consisting of hundreds of already enslaved native people and a smaller number of whites, set off for the interior, some of them backed by the Crown. *Bandeira* expeditions were especially common between 1625 and 1650 when the Dutch were making it difficult for slaves to be transported across the Atlantic from Africa, forcing the colonists to seek local people to enslave. The *bandeirantes* would attack villages, even those run by Jesuits, and seize prisoners who were brought back to the coast and sold as slaves in São Vicente and Rio de Janeiro. From there they would be transported to sugar plantations or wheat farms, mainly in the São Paulo area. At the time, wheat was particularly in demand as the Portuguese fleet had been wiped out by the Dutch, rendering it impossible to import it. This was a particular problem while there was a war being fought on Brazilian soil as there were troops who had to be fed. When the war was over, however, cheap foreign wheat once again became available, making domestic production unprofitable.

One of the principal aims of the *bandeirantes* was to find gold, an aspiration of the Portuguese since they had first set foot in the territory. Finally, in 1695, it was discovered on the Rio das Velhas, in the modern-day state of Minas Gerais. Further gold finds followed during the next fifty years in other parts of the colony and, in 1730, diamonds were discovered in the northern part of the territory. The discovery of gold re-kindled Portuguese interest in its distant colony, creating an explosion of immigrants, and around 600,000 arrived from Portugal in the first half of the eighteenth century. The Portuguese government, becoming concerned about depopulation of the homeland, restricted emigration and limited the number of clerics leaving the country. But, burdened by a trade imbalance with Britain, the gold made a difference to the Portuguese economy. Some of it did remain in Brazil while some went to the royal coffers in Lisbon to be spent by João V (r. 1706–50). The remainder fell into British hands, often illegally.

Suddenly, sugar was no longer king in Brazil and the Northeast suffered. It had already been enduring hardships in the decades prior to the discovery of gold, leading to the migration of people from the area, while increases in the price of slaves did not help. Power moved south to the port of Rio de Janeiro where slaves from Africa were unloaded and where gold was loaded onto vessels for export. Eventually, in 1763, Rio replaced Salvador as capital of Brazil.

By this time, the Portuguese Crown was taking an unprecedented interest in its South American colony, especially the tribute that had to be paid. To reduce smuggling and maximise its income, officials introduced revenue-collection systems. The royal fifth or *quintal* was introduced – a fifth of all metal that was mined was taken by the Crown. The *capitação* – a tax placed on every business in Brazil – was also levied. Those who owned slaves had to pay for every slave they owned over the age of twelve. Those who worked on their own had to pay a personal tax.

Between 1708 and 1709, there was civil unrest – known as the War of the *Emboabas* (Greenhorns' War). The *paulistas* (people of São Paulo) resented outsiders being permitted to own mining concessions. They failed in their cause but succeeded in having their area separated from Rio de Janeiro to form the new captaincy of São Paulo and Minas do Ouro. In 1711 São Paulo was declared a city and nine years later, Minas Gerais became a separate captaincy.

As was usually the case in Brazil, the great distances involved made it difficult for the Portuguese government to achieve its objectives in the area where gold had been discovered. Corruption was a major factor, added to the fact that, as we have seen, the colonial world often found it difficult to prioritise the Crown's demands over its own. Indeed, the people who began to populate this area had numerous conflicts with the Minas Gerais colonial authorities.

The gold rush in Brazil went through two distinct phases. The first, in the final years of the seventeenth century and the first years of the eighteenth, was a difficult time. The entire colony endured galloping inflation and devastating famine. Things improved through time and Minas Gerais society became wealthy, as demonstrated by the extravagant architecture of cities such as Ouro Preto, Congonhas do Campo, Sabará and Caeté. A cosmopolitan society was emerging, concentrated on cities that were being transformed into busy commercial and cultural centres. The captaincy of Minas Gerais became home to many beautiful new baroque churches.

After 1748, gold mining began to decline and within fifty years its role in the Brazilian economy was negligible. This was, of course, catastrophic for Minas Gerais and its cities. For example, in 1740, the city of Ouro Preto had 200,000 inhabitants; by 1804, only 7,000 people lived and worked there.

Slavery in Brazil

The Portuguese Crown initially resisted the enslavement of the native people, preferring, instead, to make them Christian citizens of the empire and, indeed, the papal grant that authorised Portuguese claims on Brazil stated that the Portuguese king had a duty to Christianise, civilise and even protect the natives. The Jesuits were the most active in this field, reminding the king of his duties and defending the indigenous population from external pressures. Over the years, the monarch usually supported the views of the Jesuits, rulers such as Manuel I and João III urging tolerance and understanding, even as the planters' representatives were condemning the indigenous peoples as lazy and barbaric. It was permitted to enslave any indigenous person who took up arms against the colonists, providing the colonists with an opportunity they were happy to exploit, simply claiming that their captives had been taken while fighting against them. The religious committee, the *Mesa da Consciência e Ordens* (Board of Conscience and Orders), was established in Lisbon to deal with any issues arising from these laws and, in theory, at any rate, had the authority to punish planters found to be holding indigenous people illegally. King Sebastião I (r.1557–78) confirmed the law while King Philip II (r.1598–1621) stipulated that the period during which someone captured in war could be enslaved should be limited to ten years. Philip III (r. 1621–40) ruled that all native people were free and should be paid for their labour but this was anathema to planters and lobbying and riots in Brazil forced him to rescind the law. The enslavement of indigenous people was brought to an end by a number of factors – the high death rate among them, caused by both disease and unreasonable labour demands; their retreat deeper into the interior, taking them far from the clutches of the Europeans; their gradual absorption into Brazilian society; and, critically, the rapidly increasing use of slaves imported from Africa. Finally, Sebastião José de Carvalho e Melo (1699–1782), better known as the Marques de Pombal, Secretary of State for King José I (r. 1750–1777) throughout his entire reign, and a crucial figure in Portuguese history, raised the native people of Brazil to a position of equality with the rest of the monarch's other subjects. Each was allocated a Portuguese surname, was required to speak Portuguese and was granted personal freedom. Their villages were to be given a school where Portuguese would be taught. Marriage to an Indian man or woman would bring better chances of advancement and it was made illegal to describe anyone of Indo-Portuguese ethnic background in an offensive or insulting way. It was a ruling that would have huge implications for the future of the colony and the country that it would later become. At the time, the majority of the remaining indigenous population was located in the North and that region was now integrated with the rest of the country. Of course, the exploitation of the indigenous people continued, regardless.

As the sugar industry expanded – it now accounted for 95 per cent of the colony's exports – it became obvious that the Indian was not the solution to the increasing labour shortage. The discovery of gold and diamonds in Minas Gerais in the 1690s changed the nature of Brazilian slavery, slave labour now being required to work the mines. Later, urban slavery expanded in growing cities such as Rio de Janeiro and Salvador. The Portuguese had, of course, been involved in the importation of slaves from Africa long before the discovery of Brazil and Portuguese sailors were well acquainted with the West African coast. The first slaves had arrived in Lisbon from Mauritania in 1441 and between 1441 and 1521 it is estimated that some 156,000 slaves were imported from West Africa. The transatlantic trade began around 1518, supplanting the system whereby slaves had to pass through Portugal on their way to the Americas so that tax could be levied on them. It is thought that the first shipment of people directly to Brazil was brought there from Guinea by the slave-trader Jorge Lopes Bixorda. Africans seemed to adapt well to the work and they brought none of the moral dilemmas that exploitation of the indigenous peoples did. The initial trickle of slaves from Africa soon became a flood.

Brazil exchanged tobacco, sugar, manioc flour, spirits, cloth and sweetmeats for slaves and before long states such as Angola were almost entirely dependent on the trade. By the end of the eighteenth century, the triangular trade route had been established. In this system, traders set out from the ports of half a dozen European nations for the coast of Africa where they exchanged goods for people who had been captured in the interior and force-marched to the coast. They were loaded onto ships and transported across the Atlantic – a dreadful six-to eight-week voyage known as the Middle Passage.

Everyone involved in this despicable trade had one aim and one aim only – to make as much profit as possible. In order to do that, they had to keep alive as many of their cargo as they could, and not just alive; they had to be in good condition when they arrived on the other side of the ocean so that they could be sold for the best possible price. Healthy slaves were more profitable, but keeping them healthy did not preclude the use of corporal punishment for bad behaviour and good use was made of such weapons as the 'cat o' nine tails', a multi-tailed whip that had traditionally been used as an implement of punishment in the British Royal Navy. More severe punishments were reserved for rebellious acts.

Each captain had to negotiate for the purchase of slaves and with his ship lying at anchor off the African coast, it might take as long as three months for him to assemble the three hundred or so slaves that would make the voyage worthwhile. The journey out would probably have carried manufactured goods for trade or sale. When these goods had been unloaded, therefore, the ship's carpenter had the task of installing slave decks that were no more than five feet apart between upper and lower decks. Once on board, the slaves were tightly packed below decks. Slave ship captains were either known as 'tight packers' or 'loose packers', a description that depended on how many slaves they packed into their holds. Sadly, most of them were 'tight packers', especially during the late eighteenth century. A 1788 British law permitted a vessel of 320 tons to carry 454 slaves, but one slaver of that size, the *Brookes*, is reported to have carried 609 slaves on one of her voyages.

Slaves lay in spaces that were smaller than a grave, although they would become as good as a grave for many. A document by Theophilus Conneau, a slaver who wrote about his experiences between 1829 and 1847, reported:

'At sundown, the Second Mate and Boatswain descend, cat in hand, and stow the negroes for the night. Those on the starboard side face forward, and in one another's lap, vulgarly called spoon fashion. On the port side they are stored with face aft; this position is considered preferable for the free pulsation of the heart. The tallest are selected for the greatest breadth of the vessel, while the short size and youngsters are stowed in the fore part of the ship. Great precaution is also taken to place those such as may have sores or boils on the side most convenient for their distemper... The lower deck once full, the rest are stowed on the deck which is prepared with loose boards to keep the water from under them; they are covered in fair weather with spare sails and with tarpaulins in rainy nights... This discipline of stowing them is of the greatest importance on board slavers; otherwise every Negro would accommodate himself with all the comfortability of a cabin passenger.'

Ventilation below decks was poor and disease was never far away. The stench of death mixed with those of blood, urine, vomit and human waste. Men and women were kept apart and the young tended to be housed with the female slaves. Often, in fact, the women and children were allowed to move freely during the day – better than being below decks, of course, but subjecting them, often, to the unwanted attentions of crew members.

As time passed and traders gained experience in transporting human beings, the death rate fell and in the eighteenth century it was actually 50 per cent less than it had been during the early days of the trade. During the 360-year period of the slave trade, it is estimated that the average death rate during the Middle Passage was 12.5 per cent – or 40,000 slaves a year.

Those who were intended for Brazil and survived the journey were off-loaded, sold as slaves and put to work. The ships then completed the third leg of the triangle laden with goods such as sugar, coffee, tobacco, rice, and, later, cotton, all of which had been produced by slave labour. Direct shipments also continued with twenty-four vessels a year travelling to Angola from Rio de Janeiro alone by 1800. Over the three centuries during which slaves were imported into Brazil, it is estimated that some four million Africans were transported across the Atlantic. They came from various parts of the continent – Guinea, Dahomey, Nigeria, Ghana, Cape Verde, São Tomé, Angola, the Congo, Mozambique and other places. And they could be found everywhere in the colony, working in a variety of trades as well as in the plantations and the mines. As Johan Maurits said at the time: 'It is not possible to effect anything in Brazil without slaves... and they cannot be dispensed with upon any consideration whatsoever; if anyone feels that this is wrong, it is a futile scruple.'

There were few scruples. European imperialism would have no such concerns for several centuries. The Roman Catholic Church, which had so protected the indigenous peoples, was happy to accept the enslavement of Africans as long as they were Christianised. There were some dissenting voices, such as the seventeenth-century Jesuit priest Antônio Vieira (1608–97) who denounced the treatment of African slaves and the very institution of slavery itself in a sermon he delivered in Brazil:

'Can there be a greater want of understanding, or a greater error of judgement between men and men than for me to think that I must be your master because I was born farther away from the sun, and that you must be my slave because you were born nearer to it?'

(*A History of Brazil* by E Bradford Burns, New York, Columbia University Press, 1980)

The Crown issued edicts regarding the treatment of slaves in 1688, 1698 and 1714 but there was also resistance and rebellion. Sometimes slaves rose up, killing their owners and burning their buildings and fields. They often took to their heels and disappeared into the interior, in itself a dangerous act. A number of these fugitives established settlements, known as *quilombos*, that not only provided shelter for escaped slaves, but also other minorities such as indigenous people, Jews and Arabs. The most famous of all the *quilombos* was Palmares, established around 1600 near Recife, which became an independent, self-sufficient republic. Made up of several settlements with a combined population of around 30,000, Palmares lasted for almost a century, despite repeated campaigns by the colonial authorities to shut it down. The Portuguese claimed that its inhabitants encouraged other slaves to flee and that its existence blocked agrarian expansion to the west. The men of Palmares became masters in the martial art of *capoeira*, still practised by many as a dance form in Brazil. They were finally defeated by a Portuguese artillery assault in 1694.

As in other slave-owning societies, white masters often took advantage of the black women in their charge, leading to a growing mixed race population in the colony. For example, in 1803 in the city of Salvador da Bahia, situated in the heart of sugar- and tobacco-producing country, the population of 100,000 was made up of around 30,000 whites and 30,000 people of mixed race, the remainder being black. By 1818, only about a third of the entire Brazilian population of 3.5 million could be categorised as white. 500,000 were mixed race and 2 million were black. Gold, of course, seduced many Europeans to establish a new life in Brazil and, in the course of the eighteenth century, their number increased tenfold. It is extraordinary, however, that there was comparatively little inter-racial trouble. Of course, the lives of the native peoples and the Africans were indescribably harsh but, remarkably, a homogeneous nation was being formed, inhabited by a race carved out of the cultures of three continents – Africa, Europe and South America.

The Pombaline Era

Towards the end of the eighteenth century, the Western world began to undergo a radical transformation. Since the sixteenth century, the monarchs of Europe had ruled absolutely, but a new mood began to sweep across the continent. It would develop into the Age of Enlightenment, marked by the French Revolution, the declaration of independence by Britain's colonies in North America and the advocacy of enlightened thought and liberal ideas. The Industrial Revolution was beginning in Britain, bringing new industries and new machinery, especially in the manufacture of textiles. New agricultural techniques were being introduced and British merchants were beginning to exert increasing control over international trade. Britain was on its way to becoming the most powerful nation on earth, the British imposing the free market on the world but also protecting their own markets by enforcing tariffs. They started to destabilise commerce in the Spanish and Portuguese colonies in the Americas with the use of trade agreements, smuggling and by making local arrangements with merchants.

There was a growing conviction at the time that slavery was an evil that the world could do without. In Britain and France, abolitionists began to be taken seriously and revolutionary France made slavery illegal in its colonies in 1794 although Napoleon Bonaparte (1769–1821) re-established the practice a decade later. Britain banned the importation of slaves into its colonies in 1807, the United States following suit a year later. Meanwhile, the ultra-conservative leaders of Portugal attempted to protect their Brazilian colony from the liberalising ideas flourishing across Europe by ruthlessly suppressing political dissent and banning printing presses as well as pamphlets and books that promoted the new thinking.

The absolutist approach of the Portuguese monarchs – exemplified by the long reign of João V (r.1706–1750) – was embodied in one man, Sebastião José de Carvalho e Melo,

Marquês de Pombal. Pombal was Secretary of State, effectively Prime Minister, during the reign of the weak José I and, coming to power shortly after the devastating Lisbon earthquake, launched a collection of sweeping economic reforms. By this time, Portugal was considered somewhat backward by the rest of Europe. It relied greatly on Brazil for most of its economic support but was also heavily dependent on Britain for manufactured goods as well as for protection against Spain and France. In fact, Portuguese exports were often handled by English merchants living in Portugal. There was a need for Portugal to grow its own manufacturing industry to counterbalance the inordinate expenditure of the Portuguese Crown, the cost of re-building following the earthquake, expenditure on wars with Spain for territory in Brazil and to make up for the decrease in the amount of gold and silver being extracted from Brazilian mines. To this end, Pombal increased taxation and created companies and guilds to control commercial activity and thereby raise still more revenue. Minas Gerais suffered most from the tax hikes. Tax payments had been allowed to default due to the collapse of the mining industry but, in 1788, the Portuguese Crown decided to enforce the payment of all tax arrears, creating alarm in the colony. A number of prominent citizens in the city of Ouro Preto were so outraged that in 1789 they organised a conspiracy, known as the *Inconfidência Mineira* (the Minas Conspiracy). The twenty men involved – judges, priests, landowners and even royal officials – planned a coup in which they would assassinate the new governor, creating chaos during which they would seize power, proclaiming Minas Gerais an independent republic. They were betrayed and arrested before they could put their plan in motion and all were sent into exile in Angola, apart from their leader, the army officer, Joaquim José da Silva Xavier (1746–1792), who rejoiced in the nickname *Tiradentes* (Toothpuller) because of his activities as an amateur dentist. Tiradentes, who in years to come would be recognised as a Brazilian national hero, was publicly executed in 1792. As an example to everyone, he was hanged, drawn and quartered and his head put on display on a pole in Ouro Preto. The ideas of the Enlightenment had encouraged the Minas Gerais plotters, demonstrating that despite the government's best efforts, the new thinking had arrived even in Brazil. Nonetheless, the plot had little wider importance.

The French Revolution influenced another uprising, the 1798 *Inconfidência Baiana*, also known as the Revolt of the Tailors. Graffiti on the walls of Salvador called for the violent overthrow of the monarchy and its replacement with a republic. This group of plotters also demanded social equality and an end to slavery, demands that were never going to be acceptable to the Bahian elite. Inevitably, it failed to gain any popular support and 40 instigators, the majority of whom were of mixed race or black, were soon languishing in jail. Needless to say, the few white conspirators were given more lenient punishment than their black and mixed race colleagues, four of the latter being executed in 1799.

These two conspiracies were poorly organised and easily defeated by the authorities who were convinced that the notions of liberty and equality being promulgated in Europe were bound to lead to civil unrest. They did demonstrate, however, that there were some who sought change and reminded the white elite of their worst nightmare – slave insurrection.

The British and Brazil

Britain benefited hugely from the trade in gold and diamonds in Brazil, Portugal serving merely as an intermediary in the movement of profits from Minas Gerais to the bank accounts of British merchants and the vaults of British banks. This was a consequence of the Methuen Treaty, a commercial and military agreement, signed in 1703 between England and Portugal during the War of the Spanish Succession. Portugal had initially allied with the French and the Spanish but switched sides with the signing of the treaty, allying herself with Austria, England, the United Provinces and the majority of the German states. The treaty guaranteed a British market for Portuguese wines and agricultural produce in return for providing a market for goods produced in British factories and mills. The agreement was advantageous to Britain and, moreover, prevented Portugal from competing with Britain in either manufacturing or trade. When the demand for British manufactured goods in Brazil became greater than the supply of Portuguese goods to Britain, the Portuguese Crown began to pay the deficit in gold. Thus, not only did Portugal completely miss out on the huge financial benefits brought by the Industrial Revolution, it also became dependent upon Britain. Brazil was in an equally invidious position, having not only to support the Portuguese colonial system, but also to satisfy the needs of Portuguese merchants as well as British banks. There was rampant inflation and the eventual end of the gold and diamond booms in the early nineteenth century did untold damage to the colony's economy. The flood of gold profits into Portugal had created inflation throughout the entire Portuguese empire. Furthermore, the wealth pouring into royal coffers through the 'royal fifth' or quinto, removed the monarch's reliance on the Cortes – the Portuguese parliament – for money. This led to an expansion of the royal court and a rise in the number of flunkies and hangers-on. Soon, these functionaries would be serving their royal masters in far-off Brazil.

The Portuguese Royal Family Relocates to Brazil

The circumstances that heralded the end of Brazil's three-centuries-old colonial status were remarkable, especially the comparatively peaceful manner in which the move from colony to empire was effected. After all, it took fifteen years of bitter civil war to bring an end to Spain's empire in the Americas. The

Portuguese empire collapsed after only one year of fighting and with the Portuguese royal family unexpectedly relocating from Lisbon to Brazil, taking the entire royal court with it.

Following the French Revolution in 1789, a series of wars had ensued across Europe. Portugal had allied with Spain to attack the French in the Pyrenees in the 1794 War of Roussillon, a war that went badly for the Portuguese. In 1795, the Spanish sued for peace, now allying with France against the British. Portugal was now in a quandary. Should it persevere with its century-old alliance with Britain or embrace the ideals of the revolution? The response of the regent, later João VI (r.1816–26), who was ruling in the place of his mentally ill mother Queen Maria (r.1777–1816), was to maintain Portugal's neutrality in the conflict. However, this was jeopardised by the French Emperor Napoleon's Berlin Decree of 1806 in which he proclaimed a blockade of British ports in response to Britain's blockade of French ports. This was the Continental System, devised by Napoleon to cut Britain off from trade with Europe. Portugal was given an ultimatum and, after some prevarication, Prince Regent João was forced to declare war on his erstwhile ally. By this time, however, Napoleon had other plans for Portugal, deciding that it should be partitioned. In October 1807, France and Spain signed the Treaty of Fontainebleau, breaking up the country and dividing its colonies – including Brazil, of course – between the two signatories. As the French entered Portugal in November 1807 to take control of the country, the prince regent and the entire royal family decided that, rather than be taken prisoner, they would go into what they hoped would be temporary exile in Brazil. British naval protection was provided and from 15 November, around 15,000 people – civil servants, ministers, judges, senior clergy and hangers-on – boarded some forty ships to accompany the royal personages on the voyage to Brazil. Also on board were the royal treasury, government archives and thousands of books that would become the basis of the National Library of Rio de Janeiro.

After a difficult voyage, the ship carrying the prince regent arrived at Salvador on 22 January 1808 where he stepped ashore to a warm welcome, the first European head of state to set foot in the New World. His first official act was an important one, a decree opening Brazilian ports to trade with friendly nations, thereby bringing an end to the mercantile system – the control of a colony's exports by the mother country – that had prevailed for so long. Of course, 'friendly nations' really meant Great Britain and this decision would once again prove extremely advantageous to British merchants but it had, after all, been the protection of British ships that had made the royal crossing of the Atlantic possible. Indeed, Rio de Janeiro became important in the landing of British imported goods, leading to an influx of British merchants and agents into Rio. João, of course, had more practical financial reasons for the opening of the ports. He had a pressing need to raise revenue for his court and for the colony and a great deal would come from customs duties. In addition, he wanted to eliminate the smuggling of goods into British hands. It was also a positive move for Brazilian exporters of sugar and cotton who were now free to sell to anyone.

João did not remain long in Salvador. In March, he and his retinue arrived in Rio de Janeiro which immediately became the capital of Brazil and the Portuguese empire. In an effort to modernise and breathe life into the Brazilian economy, he revoked decrees that prohibited the establishment of factories in Brazil, encouraged the introduction of new machinery, and dispensed with tariffs on raw materials that had to be imported for industrial use. Help was also provided for wool, silk and iron producers. These actions did not pass without protest from merchants both in Rio and in Lisbon. In summer 1808, therefore, João was forced to restrict free trade to a few ports only – Belém, São Luis, Recife, Salvador and Rio de Janeiro. The trade amongst colonial ports was reserved for Portuguese vessels.

Not only was the prince regent dependent upon the British to defeat the French and recover his country, he was also reliant on them to protect the Portuguese colonies. This gave him little leverage in the negotiations for the 1810 Treaty of Navigation and Commerce with Britain that set a tariff of 15 per cent on British goods imported into Brazil, even less than the tariff on Portuguese imports. Portuguese and Brazilian merchants were unable to compete and the prince regent's nascent efforts to industrialise his colony were frustrated.

Britain had turned against slavery and in the Treaty of Alliance and Friendship, a sister treaty to the Treaty of Navigation and Commerce, the Portuguese Crown promised to limit slavery and the slave trade within its borders. At the Treaty of Vienna that marked the end of the Napoleonic Wars, Portugal further agreed to end all trade in slaves north of the equator. Britain was now given the right to board vessels that were suspected of transporting slaves, but the shameful trade continued regardless and would even increase during the 1820s.

In 1815 the regent announced that Brazil would henceforward be part of the United Kingdom of Portugal, Brazil and the Algarves. Portugal, meanwhile, maintained a foreign policy from its new seat of government in Rio de Janeiro where a Ministry of War and Foreign Affairs was established. It focused its attention on the Banda Oriental territory in the River Plate region that had been disputed by Portugal and Spain for over a century. In 1811 and again in 1816, the prince regent dispatched expeditions there with the intention of seizing it for the Portuguese Crown. Eventually, the Uruguayan forces were defeated and in 1821, Banda Oriental was incorporated into Brazil, renamed the Cisplatine Province. Conflict in that area did not end, however.

Queen Maria died in 1816 and, although João took on the mantle of king, it was not until 1818 that he was thus acclaimed. He seemed to enjoy life in the tropics, but there was considerable friction between the recently arrived Portuguese and native-born Brazilians. Senior government positions rarely went to Brazilians and although a few Brazilian landowners and officials were given titles and honours, no native-born Brazilian was allowed to become a government minister or member of the Council of State that advised the ruler. Meanwhile, the Portuguese were disdainful of the colonials and longed to return to Lisbon. Brazilians came to resent their presence, a resentment that led to a revolt that began in Recife in Pernambuco in 1817. A republic was proclaimed there and demands were made that all Portuguese be expelled from the province. There was a great deal of support, even from landowners and some army officers and so many priests supported it that it has become known as the 'Revolution of Priests'. It failed to spread any further than the Northeast, however, and troops were eventually dispatched to quell the rebellion.

Even after the final defeat of Napoleon in 1815, João was reluctant to undertake the arduous sea voyage back to Lisbon, a state of affairs that helped to foment unrest in Portugal which had arrived at a moment of profound crisis. The king's absence with many of the organs of government had created a void in the running of the country, which was further complicated by a failing economy caused in part by the free trade that had benefited Brazil but had damaged Portugal's finances. Even the military was in crisis. British officers occupied many of the senior ranks and Portuguese officers were invariably passed over for promotion. In the king's absence, Portugal was governed by a regency council chaired by British Field Marshal William Beresford (1768–1856). After the defeat of Napoleon, Beresford became commander in chief of the Portuguese army.

In 1820 the uprising known as the *Revolução Liberal* (Liberal Revolution) erupted in Oporto in the north of Portugal, rapidly spreading to the rest of the country and culminating in the revolt of Lisbon. The revolutionaries called for an end to absolute monarchy, a limit on the pervasive influence of the British, greater emphasis on the interests of the bourgeoisie and more power for the *Cortes*. In January 1821, a *Cortes* was convened which, as well as drafting a new liberal constitution, demanded the return of the royal court to Lisbon in order, as they put it, 'to restore the metropolitan dignity'. In Rio, the 'Portuguese faction', consisting of military officers, bureaucrats and some merchants, pushed for the king's return, eager for Brazil once more to be subordinate to Portugal. Meanwhile, the 'Brazilian party', made up of landowners from the captaincies near Rio de Janeiro, Brazilian-born bureaucrats and merchants who were prospering from free trade, argued that João should stay where he was. Fearing the forfeiture of his throne if he failed to return, João VI capitulated, finally setting sail from Brazil, accompanied by 4,000 Portuguese, on 26 April 1821. He left behind his son, twenty-three-year-old Pedro (r.1822–31) as prince regent, ruling with the help of a council of ministers. It has been suggested that in doing this, João was acknowledging that Brazil would soon be independent anyway, and that he wanted to ensure that his son became its first ruler. The *Cortes* had other ideas, of course, and sought to restore the mercantile nature of its relationship with its colony, re-establishing Portuguese exclusivity in trade and reducing it from its status as the 'Kingdom of Brazil', re-naming it the 'Principality of Brazil'. They also demanded the return of Prince Pedro to Lisbon.

These changes were instituted long before the arrival of the Brazilian delegates to the *Cortes* amongst whom were a number of radicals who had participated in the 1817 revolution in Pernambuco, men who were fervent advocates of Brazilian independence – Cipriano Barata (1762–1838) of Bahia, Francisco Muniz Tavares (1793–1876) of Pernambuco and Antônio Carlos Ribeiro de Andrada (1773–1845) of São Paulo.

The demarcation lines created by the Treaty of Tordesillas in 1494 and the Treaty of Zaragoza of 1529 had long ceased to have any relevance; if they did, Spain would have controlled everything beyond the 46th meridian which would have placed São Paulo and everything to the west and south in Spanish hands. Brazil had crept westwards with the *bandeiras* expeditions and the requirement of cattle ranchers for new grazing. The westward expansion had been furthered by the mining expeditions of the eighteenth century and had been extended southwards by military means. Of course, such expansion had to be agreed with Spain and this had duly been done with the 1750 signing of the Treaty of Madrid in which the principle of *uti possidetis* (basically, who owns by fact, owns by right) was applied. Portugal had benefited from this, but it had given up Sacramento Colony, situated on the River Plate, close to Montevideo. In return, Spain gave Portugal the Seven Missions Territory on the Uruguai River. This failed to end the disputes about the southern boundaries and Seven Missions was returned to Spain in the 1777 Treaty of São Ildefenso.

It is estimated that around the end of the colonial period, there were roughly 3,600,000 people in Brazil, 74 per cent of them living in the Minas Gerais, Rio de Janeiro, Bahia and Pernambuco captaincies.

4

Imperial Brazil
1822 to 1889

Independence

Naturally, Brazilian landowners and merchants were concerned that the decisions taken about their territory by the *Cortes* in Lisbon would result in commercial privileges and monopolies being restored, to the benefit of the Portuguese and the detriment of Brazilians. The *Cortes*, after all, was seeking to revoke the trade agreements with Britain that, although undoubtedly favourable to the British, were also lucrative for wealthy Brazilian landowners and beneficial for Brazilian consumers generally. The *Cortes* also tried to take back control in Lisbon of many of the government offices that João had set up in Brazil. In anticipation of resistance from the colony to these changes, troops were readied for dispatch across the Atlantic and plans were made to introduce military governors who would be directly responsible to officials in Lisbon. This all changed dramatically, however, on 9 January 1822 – the day now known as *Dia de Fico* (I Shall Stay Day) – when Prince Pedro made the fateful decision to stay in Brazil. Having been presented with a petition containing the signatures of 8,000 Brazilians begging him to stay, his response was: 'Since it is for the good of all and the general happiness of the Nation, I am willing. Tell the people that I am staying.'

The previous year, Brazilian army troops under the command of Portuguese Lieutenant-General Jorge Avilez (1785–1845) had mutinied, insisting that the prince swear an oath to maintain the

Portuguese constitution. Pedro had met the rebels face-to-face and persuaded them to back down from their more radical demands, although this attempted coup d'état left him weakened. Following Pedro's decision to remain in Brazil, Avilez began to agitate once again. This time, however, the prince fought back, using troops who had remained loyal to him. Outnumbered, Avilez surrendered and he and his troops were sent into exile. Pedro then began to rebuild the Brazilian army and appointed a Brazilian, José Bonifácio de Andrada e Silva (1763–1838), Minister of the Interior and Foreign Affairs. Bonifácio became his chief political adviser. Bonifácio and his equally politically-minded brothers, Antonio Carlos (1773–1845) and Martim Francisco (1775–1844), were sons of a wealthy sugar exporter from Santos. José was a liberal conservative who supported progressive notions, such as the ending of slavery, agrarian reform and free immigration into Brazil. Importantly, he believed that Brazil should be a monarchy.

The 'Brazilian party' was now formed of two factions. The conservative wing initially favoured greater autonomy from Portugal, although it later embraced the idea of an independent Brazil, governed by a constitutional monarchy and limited elected representation. On the other, more radical wing, were those who sought a monarchy with greater popular representation and others who wanted Brazil to be an independent republic. To establish exactly what the future of the country should be, a constitutional convention was agreed upon.

Civil service officials sent from Portugal were barred from taking up office and, in August 1822, Prince Pedro announced that troops from Portugal should be considered enemies. Naturally, the *Cortes* was outraged, declaring that Pedro's decrees be revoked and insisting once again on his return to Portugal. Furthermore, Brazilian ministers were accused of treason. On 7 September 1822, Pedro received letters informing him that the *Cortes* would not accept self-governance in Brazil and that anyone disobeying its orders would be punished. Pedro is said to have climbed on his horse and announced to his entourage and his guard-of-honour, in the so-called 'cry of Ipiranga' on the shore of the Ipiranga Brook in southeastern Brazil, '*Independência ou morte!*' ('Independence or death!'):

'Friends, the Portuguese *Cortes* wished to enslave and persecute us. As of today our bonds are ended. By my blood, by my honor, by my God, I swear to bring about the independence of Brazil. Brazilians, let our watchword from this day forth be "Independence or Death!"'

(*Dom Pedro: The Struggle for Liberty in Brazil and Portugal, 1798*–1834 by Neill Macaulay, 1986, Durham, North Carolina, Duke University Press)

Thus was Brazil's independence formalised and on 1 December 1822, the twenty-four-year-old prince regent was crowned Pedro I, the 'Constitutional Emperor and Perpetual Defender of Brazil'. The title of emperor had been chosen so as not to offend his father King João VI of Portugal who was still revered by many Brazilians. The immense size of the country also suggested that it was more of an empire than a kingdom.

Unlike the nations of Spanish America, therefore, that had become republics on independence, Brazil became a monarchy. For the Brazilian elite, republicanism was synonymous with social and political instability and there was never the slightest chance that Brazil would be anything other than a monarchy, especially as there was a royal prince in the country who had already been ruling. Indeed, the presence in Rio de Janeiro of an existing administration meant that there was little change, apart from the fact that Brazilians began to take the places of Portuguese in senior positions in the government and administration.

The Creation of a Brazilian State

Pedro I followed the lead of most European rulers of the time, choosing to rule as a constitutional monarch, which necessitated a constitution. The task of creating one was given to a Constituent and Legislative General Assembly of ninety indirectly elected members that first met in Rio de Janeiro on 3 May 1823. The debates were fractious and inconclusive. Those who sided with the emperor favoured what was described as 'centralism', claiming that the nation would be best served by a powerful executive, namely the monarch. Delegates with more liberal tendencies expressed a fear that this might lead to absolutism. Eventually, on 11 November 1823, following the resignation of José Bonifácio due to the failure to agree and Pedro's suspicion that his powers were in danger of being restricted, the emperor dissolved the assembly. He claimed that he feared that elements of it, led by the Bonifácio brothers, were preparing to launch a revolution. The brothers were arrested and exiled, and on 25 March 1824 Pedro appointed a *Conselho de Estado* (Council of State) to draft a constitution.

This constitution provided for a highly centralised state with the country separated into eighteen provinces administered by a national government. Although executive power would lie, of course, in the hands of the emperor, there would be a legislature consisting of a General Assembly made up of a Senate and a Chamber of Deputies. Those appointed to the Senate – they were to be chosen by the emperor – would serve as senators for life, whereas deputies would serve four-year terms and would be elected. The franchise, however, was limited, as during colonial times, to those adult males who qualified on grounds of property or income. The emperor was given substantial powers and, if things were not proceeding as he wished, he could at any time dissolve the Chamber of Deputies and call for new elections using what was termed 'moderating power' in article 98 of the Constitution. Roman Catholicism would continue to be the national religion of Brazil and there would be a Brazilian nobility – prominent individuals with titles given by the emperor. In order to prevent the emergence of a 'blood aristocracy', these would not be hereditary.

Although welcomed by the wealthy elite of Rio de Janeiro, São Paulo and Minas Gerais, such a system was anathema to groups in the Northeast who still mourned the end of the relationship with Portugal. After all, while Brazil was a colony, the Northeast enjoyed better communications with Lisbon than with the cities of the south. Rebellious elements in Ceará, Paraíba and Pernambuco attempted to secede from the new empire and create an independent republic known as the Confederation of the Equator. The rebellion was quickly suppressed by imperial forces led by General Luís Alves de Lima e Silva (1803–1880) – later Duke of Caxias – and the British Admiral Thomas Cochrane (1775–1860) who was commander of the Brazilian Navy. Nonetheless, rebellions would continue in Pernambuco until 1848.

In 1825, Banda Oriental in the south declared itself independent of Brazil, the rebels creating the United Provinces of the River Plate, incorporating modern-day Uruguay. This led to the Cisplatine War fought between Brazil and Argentina in December of that year, a war that although financially ruinous for both combatants, would prove particularly disastrous for Brazil. Eventually, Britain stepped in, anxious to restore commercial activity disrupted by the conflict, to mediate a peace agreement that resulted in Brazil losing territory and the establishment of Uruguay as an independent nation.

The 24-year-old emperor who had to deal with such problems was a talented young man, given that his education had been seriously neglected when he was a child. He was regarded as something of a hero in Brazil but began to gain a rather dubious reputation as a result of his amorous escapades. His popularity declined because of his bad treatment of his first wife, Maria Leopoldina of Austria (1797–1826), daughter of the Holy Roman

Emperor Francis II (r.1792–1806). Pedro lived openly and scandalously with his beautiful mistress, Domitila de Castro (1797–1867) with whom he had five illegitimate children and on whom he bestowed the title 'Marquesa de Santos'. His popularity was further damaged by enforced military conscription during the Cisplatine War, but his problems were compounded in the second half of the 1820s by a damaging increase in the cost of living, the result of the issue by the government of copper coinage. The situation was further complicated by a fall in the exchange rate of the Brazilian currency. Native-born Brazilians blamed Portuguese merchants who controlled much of the retail trade and whom they accused of rampant profiteering. Pedro, they claimed, favoured Portuguese interests and surrounded himself with his compatriots at court. Dissatisfaction grew and there was even a rumour that he was about to overthrow the constitution in order to effect a return to absolute rule. Demonstrations broke out in Rio de Janeiro and a radical liberal faction known as the *exaltados* (exalteds or zealots) was highly critical of the emperor. The *exaltados* opposed Portuguese influence in the empire and campaigned for the establishment of a federal republic.

Many of the Brazilian elite had supported Pedro because they feared liberalism or because they were afraid of losing their positions in the government, but soon even they were beginning to change sides. Their suspicion of the emperor's motives were heightened when, in March 1826, his father, João VI, died, leaving Pedro, as the late king's oldest son, as heir to the Portuguese throne. Soon, the emperor was unable even to rely on the support of his army. His soldiers – mostly men of mixed race who endured a harsh regime – were dismayed by recent military failures, blaming them on their Portuguese-born officers. In summer 1830, restlessness increased with news of the overthrow of the French King Charles X (r. 1824–30) and the beginning of the liberal July Monarchy. In March 1831, Pedro tried to reduce anti-Portuguese feeling by appointing a cabinet made up of Brazilian-born moderates but a month later he replaced them with his own men. People again took to the streets, demanding the dismissal of what was called the 'ministry of marquises' and the reinstatement of the former cabinet. The emperor remained inflexible, famously saying, 'I will do everything for the people and nothing by the people'. He was unwilling to give up his constitutional power to appoint ministers. But, when some of Pedro's most senior officers withdrew their support from him, he was left with only one option – abdication. On 7 April 1831, Brazil's first emperor, Pedro I, abdicated in favour of his five-year-old son, Pedro II (r. 1831–89), telling his people:

'I prefer to descend from the throne with honour rather than go on reigning as a sovereign who has been dishonoured and degraded. Those born in Brazil no longer want me for the reason that I am Portuguese... My son has the advantage over me in that he is a Brazilian by birth. The Brazilians respect him. He will have no difficulty in governing, and the constitution will guarantee him his rights. I renounce the Crown with the glory of ending as I began – constitutionally.'

(Document quoted in *A History of Brazil* by E Bradford Burns, New York, Columbia University Press, 1980)

Pedro departed for Europe aboard the British ship HMS *Volage*, leaving his young heir behind. It would be a while, though, before Pedro II would take the throne. Article 121 of the 1824 Constitution stipulated that a monarch could not ascend the throne until he reached the age of eighteen. This would not be until December 1843. In the end, he came to power earlier than that, but it would still be ten years before he would become emperor. In the meantime, a regency was put in place.

The Regency Period

During the Regency Period, Brazil was governed by politicians acting in Pedro II's name. It was a period of great unrest during which the empire's territorial cohesiveness was severely put to the test and centralisation and the role of the armed forces monopolised political debate. The regents made efforts to introduce reforms that would remove the stigma of absolutism but although these were often aimed at securing individual rights and liberalising the political system, they served only to foment even more unrest, especially amongst the ruling elite.

The first regents, elected by the General Assembly, were General Francisco de Lima e Silva (1785–1853), José da Costa Carvalho (1796–1860), from Bahia and João Braulio Moniz (1796–1835) of Maranhão. In 1834, it was decided to replace this unwieldy three-man regency with a single regent, to be elected every four years. The first person to hold this position was Father Diogo Antônio Feijó (1784–1843), a liberal priest from São Paulo who defeated Holanda Cavalcanti (1797–1863), a landowner from Pernambuco in the election for the post. Feijó was a supporter of federalism and early in his regency the *Acto Adicional* (Additional Act) was passed that allowed provinces to convene local assemblies with powers to raise taxes and set expenditure. This legislation also devolved responsibility for the appointment and dismissal of local officials to provincial governments and the Council of State set up by Pedro I was abolished. Much of the legislation passed during the Regency further reduced the power of the monarchy and diminished the influence of the military. The Criminal Justice Code of 1832 gave greater power to justices of the peace, permitting them to arrest and try people accused of minor crimes, and the jury system was introduced for the majority of cases. Additionally, the right of *habeas corpus* was brought into being for those illegally jailed or whose right to freedom was endangered.

These actions failed to bring stability to Brazil. Instead, rivalry between political groupings in the regions increased, leading to violence amongst the poorer classes. Brazil was suddenly threatened with the disintegration of its national unity and, for a time, looked like it might go the way of Spanish America. The three-man regency had already had to deal with a serious threat in July 1831 when the army had mutinied in Rio de Janeiro. The revolt lasted ten days but the government, stubbornly refusing to give in to the rebels' demands, undertook a policy of reducing the number of troops by half to just over 6,000. This force was backed up by a National Guard, a body of armed citizens, established in 1831 and consisting of males between the ages of 21 and 60 who were entitled to vote in primary elections. As this exempted them from conscription into the military, damage was done to the army's strength.

Next, there was trouble in the provinces. The so-called War of the *Cabanos* broke out in the south of Pernambuco in 1832. The conservative *Cabanadas* sought to overthrow the regency and reinstate Pedro I on the Brazilian throne. Adding fuel to the fire were the prevailing economic conditions – stagnant foreign trade, a decline in the price of sugar and, as ever, the favourable tariffs given to British merchants. With the entry of increasing numbers of slaves and indigenous people into the rebellion, the issue of racial discrimination also began to rear its ugly head. The rebellion was finally suppressed in 1835 after three years of guerrilla war. The previous year, one of the principal motivations for the rebellion had been removed when Pedro I died of tuberculosis in Lisbon. As the struggle in Pernambuco limped to a close, another broke out in Belém. Slaves and poor people erupted in a revolt known as the *Cabanagem* against the rich white elite following disagreements over the presidency of the province of Pará. As many as 40,000 – 20 per cent of the province's population – lost their lives in the ensuing violence. There were uprisings in the next few years in Bahia with the Revolt of the *Males* (Muslim slaves) and Salvador with the uprising known as the *Sabinada*. Salvador was recaptured from the rebels after a blockade of its harbour and a siege lasting four months. A more serious rebellion broke out in Maranhão in December 1838. Violence was at first directed at wealthy Portuguese merchants but soon the rebels had assembled a substantial army of more than 10,000 that took the city of Caxias in July 1839. The government became increasingly concerned at the threat posed by this uprising and in 1840 Colonel Luis de Lima e Silva led a force of 8,000 troops into the region to restore order, his victory over the rebels earning him the title Duke of Caxias and the sobriquet the 'Iron Duke'. Meanwhile, an even greater threat came from the long-lasting *Farroupilha* Revolution, the uprising that finally persuaded the government that the only way to prevent such incidents was to rush through the coronation of the young emperor-elect. The revolt was started in Rio Grande do Sul in 1835 by rebels known to their opponents as *Farrapos* (ragamuffins) probably in reaction to the fact that Rio Grande do Sul was somewhat poorer than the rest of the country, sales of its main product *charque* (dried and salted beef) having suffered badly from competition from Argentinean and Uruguayan producers. They had free access to Brazilian markets while Rio Grande do Sul producers had to pay high taxes when they sold their product on the domestic market. Thus, although they were known as 'ragamuffins', the *farrapos* included in their number landowners and wealthy ranchers. They captured Porto Alegre in September 1835 and a year later declared the establishment of a Riograndense Republic. They invaded the adjacent region of Santa Catarina and proclaimed the Republic of Piratini. Finally, in 1845, the venture was terminated by the Ponche Verde Treaty that brought Rio Grande do Sul and Santa Catarina back into the Brazilian Empire.

Just two years into his regency, Father Feijó resigned, under pressure from the Conservative Party, a coalition formed in 1836 of moderates, centralists and those who had campaigned for the reinstatement of Pedro I. 'I cannot bear the ingratitude, injustice and knavery', he wrote bitterly. His resignation brought the reversal of the policy of de-centralisation. Instead, a policy known as the *Regresso* (Regression) was instituted. This was bolstered in April 1838 by the election of a *Regresso* or Conservative as regent to succeed Feijó. Pedro de Araújo Lima (1793–1870) was a plantation owner from Pernambuco who was Speaker of the Chamber of Deputies and would later be ennobled as the Marquis of Olinda. One of the first expressions of the *Regresso*, as the period became known, was the 1840 Interpretive Law that brought less regional autonomy and a reduction in the power of local administrations to appoint officials. In 1841, the criminal code was amended to restore to the centre the power to appoint judges and senior police officers.

Meanwhile, the young emperor-in-waiting was regarded as a vital national symbol and was being educated by eminent men, including his father's former adviser José Bonifácio. Indeed, Pedro was reported to be unusually mature for his age, a fact stressed by Liberal politicians who, citing separatist revolts taking place in the North, Northeast and South, unexpectedly began to campaign for the elevation of the fourteen-year-old to the throne, four years in advance of the age at which the 1824 Constitution had stipulated. It represented recognition of the failure of the Regency to govern effectively. In July 1840, Araujo Lima resigned and Pedro II was offered the Crown.

The Second Empire

The coronation of Emperor Pedro II on 18 July 1841 was a significant moment for Brazil, symbolising the country's belief in the institution of monarchy and a reaffirmation of the nation's ongoing unity. It also brought to a conclusion the rebellious period that had begun in Pernambuco in 1817. There were further uprisings, of course. Maranhão underwent the *Balaiada* uprising in 1840, federalists rebelled in São Paulo and Minas Gerais the same year and the *farrapos* rebelled in the South in 1845. The series of revolutions that occurred in Europe in 1848 stimulated further uprisings. In Pernambuco there was a rebellion in favour of land reform and federalism called the *Praieira* revolt (named after Rua da Praia, a street in Recife). It was suppressed a year later, marking the end of separatist agitation in Brazil and signifying the increasing authority of the national government.

Brazil was now a parliamentary constitutional monarchy, not unlike that of Britain. The difference was that Pedro II still had at his disposal the useful tool of moderating power, permitting him to dismiss a government and allocate power to whichever political party he favoured at any given time. The Council of State was restored in 1841 and, like the Senate, was populated with members of the elite landowning class favoured by Pedro. By and large, however, the scholarly Pedro II showed no sign of wanting to be an autocratic ruler. He avoided party politics, but was keenly interested in government. 'I judge that the head of the executive power, in order to direct the use of that power,' he wrote, 'has the right to watch actively over the conduct of the ministry.' (Quoted in *Citizen Emperor: Pedro II and the Making of Brazil 1825–91*, Roderick J Barman, Stanford, Stanford University Press, 1999)

Brazil now enjoyed a two-party system with the Conservatives and the Liberals opposing each other. Conservative supporters were to be found amongst the landowning elite of the Northeast, the coffee planters of Rio de Janeiro, Portuguese-born merchants and government officials. They were in favour of the monarchy and centralisation and shared a desire for the preservation of slavery with the sugar planters of the Northeast. The Liberals relied on the landowners and planters of São Paulo, Minas Gerais and Rio Grande, the urban middle class and Brazilian-born merchants. Despite having been in favour of federalism in the 1830s, they had campaigned for Pedro's early coronation and now gave their approval to steps to reduce regional autonomy. In fact, there was little to choose between the two parties which undeniably had one thing in common – a fear of revolution.

After Pedro's coronation, the Liberals took control of the cabinet but, within a year, the new emperor dismissed them and asked the Conservatives to form a government. Anxious to ensure that they also had sufficient seats in the Chamber of Deputies, he called a new election. Thus, he instigated a policy of alternating governing parties, doing it no fewer than eleven times during his reign. In the forty-nine years of the Second Empire, there were thirty-six cabinets. It sounds like a policy guaranteed to create instability but remarkably it worked in the opposite way. Each of the political parties, knowing that it would be in power again before long, was prepared to wait its turn. The system also brought benefit to the emperor, because it prevented the establishment by the parties of national political powerbases. Of course, political debate was all but non-existent but this did not stop the Brazilian elite from boasting of a democratic system that allowed freedom of speech and free and open political debate in the press, just as in Britain and France. Furthermore, they claimed, issues could be put before the public for them to decide in national elections. Of course, this was far from the truth and, in fact, there was very little difference between the Conservatives and the Liberals while restrictions on who could vote in elections imposed by rural political bosses known as *coronéis* (colonels) meant that voting was rigorously controlled. Rather than creating political debate about the issues of the day, elections were simply about ensuring that the Chamber of Deputies was composed of members who would be supportive of whatever government the emperor had chosen.

Coffee

One of the things that kept Brazil unified as one nation was slavery. The provinces feared that if they seceded from the empire they would become less able to withstand the pressure from the international anti-slavery movement being spearheaded by the British. The proliferation of coffee planting brought an even greater demand for slaves. The first coffee bushes were planted in 1727 in the state of Pará by Francisco de Melo Palheta (1670–c1750). By 1770, coffee had reached Rio de Janeiro, produced initially for domestic consumption. In the Paraíba River valley that stretches across a part of Rio de Janeiro and São Paulo, conditions were found to be ideal for the cultivation of coffee plants and that was where it found its commercial impetus. Transport was good and it was close to the port of Rio de Janeiro from where it could be exported to Europe. The ranches that were established used slave labour and were based on the traditional Brazilian large-scale format. Land occupied by settlers was swallowed up, often by force and influence wielded by members of the wealthy elite. In truth, only those who already had sufficient resources could plant coffee. Significant investment had to be made in felling trees, preparing the land, buying slaves and building quarters to house them; but added to that was the fact that a coffee bush only became productive four years after planting. Planters gave little thought to the future; when one patch of soil was exhausted, the planter simply moved on to sow another patch. Prior to picking, there was little work to be done apart from weeding. Then, bushes were picked by hand by slaves who each had between 4,000 and 7,000 coffee plants to look after, which meant that little was done in terms of maintenance of the plants. Once picked, the crop was transported to the docks by mule trains that were received by intermediaries known as commissioners who sold it to exporters.

As today, Brazilian coffee production depended on the export market and European demand flourished between the 1830s and the 1850s. The United States became the biggest importer of Brazilian coffee. Britain, a resolutely tea-drinking nation, was never a big importer and what coffee it did drink mostly came from its own Caribbean colonies, from Central America and southern Asia. This brought difficulties for the Brazilian economy. Its past dependence on the British meant that much of its foreign debt was with British banks and it was still reliant on the British for credit and loans. Now it did not do enough business with Britain to service its debt or pay for its imports.

Coffee was critical to the Brazilian economy, accounting for around 18 per cent of its total export revenue. Later, between 1881 and 1890, it amounted to 61 per cent. It came in handy. In the Centre-South, increasingly the economic hub of Brazil, ports were modernised, transportation and communications were improved and jobs were created. The coffee barons, planters and landowners of the region became wealthy men, often ennobled by the emperor. But the national government guaranteed that specific regional interests were not shown favouritism by ensuring that provincial presidents did not automatically come from the local elite. Nonetheless, by the mid-nineteenth century the elite were doing sufficiently well to be enthusiastically supportive of the empire.

The Abolition of Slavery

Slavery was an issue that would not go away during the Second Empire. By the time Pedro II was crowned, only a handful of countries in the West had failed to abolish it. The wealthy, as well as many from humbler backgrounds, owned slaves. They believed slavery to be essential to the Brazilian economy and even that slaves added to their social status. As a British mineralogist noted while on a visit to Rio de Janeiro in 1828, '... slaves form the income and support of a vast number of individuals who hire them out as people in Europe do horses and mules'. (Quoted in *The Destruction of Brazilian Slavery*, 1850–88, Robert Conrad, Berkeley, University of California Press, 1972) The more intense the pressure from internal or foreign abolitionists, the more determined, it seemed, was the Brazilian 'slavocracy' to preserve the institution.

The main issue during the first half of the nineteenth century, however, was not that of ownership of slaves; it was the continuation of the transatlantic slave trade between Africa and Brazil. In 1826, pressured by the British, Brazil promised to stop the trade by 1829. It did not happen. In 1831 a law was passed that outlawed the trade, but little attention was paid to it. Indeed, the number of slaves enduring the perilous Middle Passage doubled in the following decade. But, by 1840, there was growing concern about slavery, although not entirely on grounds of morality. The Northeast was experiencing slave rebellions and unrest while outbreaks of yellow fever and cholera were being blamed on slaves. British pressure on Brazil was increasing. British vessels were now entering Brazilian waters and seizing slave-carrying ships. Finally, in 1850, the Eusébio de Queiros law – named for the politician who proposed it – was passed, not only making it illegal to import slaves into Brazil, but also providing measures to enforce the legislation. This law gave momentum to the Brazilian abolition movement, leading to support for a gradual emancipation of slaves over a period of time. Abolition became an even more pressing topic when the American Civil War brought an end to slavery in the United States in 1865, leaving Brazil in the invidious position of being the largest slave-owning country in the world.

Amongst Brazil's most vocal abolitionists were Pernambuco writer and statesman Joaquim Nabuco (1849–1910) and journalist and orator José do Patrocinio (1854–1905) from Rio de Janeiro who co-founded the Brazilian Anti-Slavery Society in 1880. But, apart from the abolitionists, there were also political moves that contributed to the end of slavery. In 1868, when the Liberal prime minister was forced to resign, his embittered party published a manifesto demanding radical changes including the abolition of slavery. The emperor had, in fact, signalled his approval of abolition the previous year but was in favour of a gradual process. He was supportive of the 1871 Law of Free Birth, also known as the Law of the Free Womb, that was aimed at giving freedom to all newborn children of slaves and slaves of the state or Crown. They would be cared for by slave-owners until the age of twenty-one or would be turned over to the state and their owners would be compensated. If the compensation was declined the child would have to work for his or her owner until the age of twenty-one at which time they would be freed. The law also allowed slaves to purchase their freedom at the prevailing market price. In effect, only a very few benefited from the law and little would change for the next twenty-one years. A debate began as to whether this time should be shortened, the Conservatives favouring the emperor's gradual approach, the Liberals seeking an end to slavery as soon as possible. But circumstances began to change. The number of slaves actually began to go down as they were freed by their owners or their freedom was bought by others. Moreover, not only was it increasingly felt that slavery was morally wrong, people also began to find that it was no longer economically viable, that wage or free labour was better in every way for all concerned. Thus, the provinces of Ceará and Amazonas freed all their slaves in 1884 and a year later, the Saraiva-Cotegipe law gave all slaves their freedom when they reached the age of sixty. By this time, abolitionists were encouraging slaves to flee the plantations which led to the army being enlisted to help round them up. Soldiers, however, were reluctant to be involved. By 1887, there were less than a million slaves. It was apparent to everyone that the shameful institution's days were at last numbered.

On 13 May 1888, the *Lei Áurea* (Golden Law), the legislation that officially ended three hundred years of slavery in Brazil, was authored by Rodrigo Augusto da Silva (1833–89) who was at the time Minister of Agriculture and a member of the Chamber of Deputies. At the time of its passing, Pedro II was convalescing in Europe following a serious illness, leaving Princess Dona Isabel – acting as regent in her father's absence – to sign the Golden Law after its approval by the Brazilian General Assembly. With this signature, all of Brazil's remaining slave population, by this time numbering around 650,000, were given their freedom.

The Paraguayan War and the 'Military Question'

Brazilian participation in the Paraguayan War of 1864–70 had dire consequences for the country. It is a war that has become notorious for causing more deaths in proportion to the number of people who fought in it than any other war in history. It also created a new generation of junior officers who differed from those who had gone before. They were educated men – very often having attended universities abroad – who had less regard for the monarchy than their predecessors.

Uruguay had come into existence in 1828 after three years of conflict between Argentina, Brazil and the faction seeking independence for the region. The British, with financial and commercial interests in the River Plate estuary, were very pleased to see the creation of a country that they hoped would bring stability to the region. The nineteenth century brought unrest, however, as Uruguay's two political parties – the Colorado, linked to business interests and Europe, and the Blanco, made up of rural landowners who opposed European influence – vied for power, often violently. Meanwhile, the inhabitants of the old Spanish province of Paraguay had overthrown their Spanish administration in 1811. In 1842, President Carlos Antonio López (1792–1862) declared himself dictator and in 1862 his son, Francisco Solano López (1827–70), came to power following his father's death. That year he entered into an alliance with the Blanco Party that ruled Uruguay at the time. Fighting broke out between the Blancos and Colorados and spilled over into Rio Grande do Sul in southern Brazil, spurring the Brazilians to invade Uruguay in order to help the Colorados seize power. The Uruguayans captured a Brazilian ship and then invaded the Mato Grosso region in western Brazil. In 1865, the Paraguayans planned to invade Uruguay but this would involve them in crossing Argentinean territory. Subsequently, on 1 May, Argentina, Brazil and Uruguay entered into a Triple Alliance and declared war on Paraguay. The

Paraguayans did not attack Uruguay as planned and all the fighting actually took place in Paraguay itself.

Brazil was not prepared for war although its navy, consisting of a few warships, easily defeated the tiny Paraguayan navy. Its army, consisting of only 18,000 poorly trained fighting men, had long been neglected. The desperate Brazilian government promised slaves their freedom if they enlisted. Finally, in 1866, the Brazilian army invaded Paraguay but was defeated in its first engagement at the Battle of Curupayty. In summer 1867, however, the Duke of Caxias led the siege and capture of the important fortress at Humaitá in southern Paraguay. The capital was taken a short while later. Brazil would occupy Paraguay until 1878.

The war was costly for Brazil. It brought a steep rise in inflation and the empire's foreign debt increased. The most telling consequence was the effect on the army. Its prestige and influence, as well as its size, were greatly increased by the conflict. The officers, whose number increased from 1,500 to 10,000, were now politicised but were uncomfortable with what appeared to be an anti-military stance emanating from the emperor. Indeed, he had deliberately eschewed the *caudilho*, military style of leadership that was popular amongst many Spanish-American rulers and was careful not to appoint military men to high-ranking political positions. The officer corps' disquiet was increased by the enforced resignation of the Liberal Prime Minister, Zacarias de Góis e Vasconcelos (1815–77), whose direction of the war effort had been to their liking. Only the fact that the military commander Caxias remained loyal to Pedro eased their feelings of discontent. His death in 1880, therefore, was a blow not only to the emperor personally, but had grave implications for the future of the monarchy.

The junior officers' irritation at the failure of the government to improve army pay and conditions developed into a feeling of political disenchantment and the beginnings of a movement to reform Brazil's political system. Officers were barred from political activity but in 1879 a group of officers publicly criticised a proposal before the General Assembly to cut the size of the army. No action was taken against them but in the coming years when officers again engaged in political debate, they would be disciplined.

The 'military question', as it was known, became a source of growing tension between the army and the government. The unrest soon spread to senior officers who demonstrated support for their younger colleagues. The main spokesman was Marshal Manuel Deodoro da Fonseca (1827–92) who, in 1887, was elected first president of Brazil's *Club Militar* (Military Club), a society created to uphold soldiers' rights. Tension rose when, in June 1889, Emperor Pedro appointed a Liberal, the Viscount of Ouro Preto (1836–1912), as prime minister. Ouro Preto wasted no time in antagonising Deodoro by naming an opponent of his as president of Rio Grande do Sul.

The Military Coup of 1889

For some time, Republican politicians had been cultivating friendships with the military, realising that as neither elections nor the General Assembly were likely to bring the empire to an end it would take the support of the army to do so. In 1887, Marshal Deodoro wrote to the emperor, warning him about his attitude towards the Brazilian military and indicating to him that the ongoing support of the army could not be guaranteed. Meanwhile, his fellow officers were eager to replace the empire with a republic, amongst them men such as Benjamin Constant (1836–1891), like Deodoro a veteran of the Paraguayan War. Meanwhile, Pedro II was suffering from diabetes and, although only 64, was becoming increasingly frail. He seemed to have lost interest in the business of government and it has been suggested that he had already accepted that the empire would not survive his death. The fact that he had no male heir suggested that he had good reason to fear for the empire's survival. His daughter, Princess Isabel (1846–1921), who had already courted controversy with her support for abolitionism, was the legal heir, but it was highly unlikely that a male-dominated society like Brazil would be prepared to accept a woman on the throne. As if it was not bad enough that she was a woman, her husband, Prince Gaston, Count of Eu (1842–1922), was French.

There was a growing feeling in Brazil that too much power was vested in the emperor, the Senate and the Council of State, none of whom, after all, had been elected. As republican clamour grew, Ouro Preto introduced measures to reduce the power of the Council of State, the General Assembly and the provincial presidents, but they were thrown out by the General Assembly. The emperor responded to this setback in the customary manner, by dissolving the General Assembly and calling for new elections to be held in November 1889. It was obvious that nothing was likely to change. The military responded by ordering Benjamin Constant, in concert with Republicans such as Quintino Bocaiúva (1836–1912) and Rui Barbosa (1849–1923), to devise plans for a coup. Early in the morning of 15 November 1889, troops commanded by Deodoro, who had agreed to be the coup's leader, surrounded government buildings in Rio de Janeiro. It was initially supposed that the action was intended simply to change the cabinet, but that afternoon Deodoro declared that Pedro II had been overthrown and that Brazil would henceforth be a republic.

That day, Pedro was at his summer palace at Petrópolis, outside Rio de Janeiro. After hurrying back to the capital, he was ordered to leave Brazil within twenty-four hours, taking the rest of the royal family with him. On 17 November, he sailed into exile in Portugal and France, choosing this fate rather than subject Brazil to an inevitable civil war. All proceeded peacefully, although many observers were astonished at the lack of support for the monarchy. Robert Adams Jr (1849–1906), United States Minister to Brazil at the time of the coup, wrote that it was 'the most remarkable ever recorded in history. Entirely unexpected by the Government or people, the overthrow of the Empire has been accomplished without bloodshed, without riotous proceedings or interruptions to the usual avocations of life'.

5

The First Republic
1889 to 1930

Immigration

In 1819, the population of Brazil had been 4,600,000, of whom 800,000 were indigenous people. By 1872, there were almost 10,000,000 Brazilians and in 1890, a census recorded 14,300,000. People of mixed race made up 42 per cent of the population, whites 38 per cent and blacks 20 per cent, the proportion of whites having increased from its 1819 figure of 30 per cent due to immigration. Coffee planters had encouraged European immigrants to come to Brazil and there were initiatives to attract German and Swiss migrants to colonise and farm sparsely populated rural areas in the South. Between 1823 and 1830 around 10,000 Europeans immigrated to Brazil, about 6,000 of whom – mostly Germans – settled in Rio Grande do Sul. Unfortunately, however, many of the settlements failed and were abandoned. When attempts were made in 1847 to use German and Swiss immigrants as plantation workers, the Europeans were dismayed by the poor wages and conditions as well as the lack of equality they were accorded. Consequently, they either established their own farms or moved to jobs in the cities. In the 1870s, there was a major wave of immigration, the 1850s figure of 10,000 immigrants a year doubling and still rising in the following decade as the abolition of slavery forced landowners and coffee planters to look elsewhere for cheap labour. In 1887, immigration from Europe reached the record high of 55,000, a figure that doubled in 1888 by which time, with slavery now abolished, the jobs in the fields of the São Paulo coffee plantations were being taken by Italian immigrants. The number of European immigrants increased in the following years with promotional initiatives such as the provincial government of São Paulo paying their fare across the Atlantic.

After abolition, while many slaves headed for the cities to find employment, many were still tied to their plantations by debt and this helped to perpetuate slavery. There remained a reluctance amongst the white elite to allow women, former slaves, the poor – whether rural or urban – and the small middle class to participate in the running of their society. The only signs of discontent at the status quo were amongst newly freed people and recently arrived immigrants, especially those living in Brazil's expanding urban areas.

Estados Unidos do Brazil (United States of Brazil)

The leaders of the coup of 1889 immediately established their regime as a 'provisional' government, declaring Brazil a federal republic. They issued proclamations justifying their action, claiming that they had undertaken the coup on behalf of the Brazilian people. Deodoro was in charge as 'chief of the provisional government' and a number of prominent politicians quickly rallied to his cause, including Rui Barbosa, Quintino Bocaiúva and Benjamin Constant, who were each rewarded with a position in the new government. Rui accepted the position of Finance Minister, Constant was appointed Minister for War and Quintino took office as Minister of Foreign Relations. The formal name of the country was changed from the Empire of Brazil to the Republic of the United States of Brazil and a new national flag was designed. Work began on a new constitution, the aim being to transform Brazil into a modern, industrial democracy.

The new constitution advocated a federal political system, fulfilling the objectives of a Republican manifesto of 1870 that had demanded the transfer of power from the centre to the regions, a move welcomed by the influential coffee industry, especially in São Paulo. As in the days of the Empire, however, there would still be a central executive administration, with a national legislature based in Rio de Janeiro. The Liberals considered this to be the best way of maintaining national unity and merchants and businessmen hoped it would help create a domestic market. It was decided to follow the political model of the United States, with a president and a federal government made up of executive, legislative and judicial bodies. The president would be elected by the people for a four-year term and would be prohibited from serving consecutive terms. The franchise was limited to literate males over the age of twenty-one, representing about 17 per cent of the population. A large majority of the Brazilian people were still unable to participate in the choice of their ruler. The rest of the world was expanding the franchise, but Brazil, still afraid of the will of the people, was reluctant to follow the trend.

Legislative power was placed in the hands of a National Congress which, like its imperial predecessor, the General Assembly, would consist of a Chamber of Deputies and a Senate. Each state was allocated three senators, each of whom would serve nine years before standing for re-election. The deputies would serve terms of three years and would be elected on the basis of population, the more highly populated states benefiting most from this, of course. Inevitably, elections were rigged. Voters in rural areas were forced to vote for the chosen candidates of the local oligarch – an abuse known as *coronelismo*. If all else failed, the election results could still be changed by Congress's Verification of Powers Commission as the election authorities in the *República Velha* (Old Republic), were not independent from the executive and the legislature and those were, of course, controlled by the ruling elite.

The twenty provinces that had existed under the empire became twenty-one with the creation of the new Federal District of the city of Rio de Janeiro. Each was permitted to create its own constitution and be self-governing, with directly elected governors and their own legislative assemblies and courts. They were given financial autonomy with the power to levy taxes on exports, this being particularly welcomed by São Paulo and Minas Gerais, two states with lucrative export economies. States were permitted to establish their own militias or police forces and São Paulo even had its own army which was every bit as well-equipped as the national army.

Church and state were separated, meaning that Brazil no longer had a state religion. The state assumed many of the responsibilities formerly held by the church – only civil marriages would be officially recognised and cemeteries were taken over by municipalities. These measures were a reflection of the beliefs of the republican leaders but also brought the many Lutheran immigrants in Brazil into the national fold. To further embrace its immigrant population, the government passed a measure decreeing that unless they expressed a wish otherwise, all foreigners who had been in Brazil on 15 November when the Brazilian Republic came into being would automatically be considered Brazilian citizens.

Generally speaking, the power lay not only with the newly politicised professional military class but also in the hands of the planter elite based mainly in the coffee-producing regions of São Paulo and the commercial and banking interests concentrated in the cities of Rio de Janeiro, São Paulo and Minas Gerais. For most people little changed but army officers probably benefited more than most with increased salaries and lucrative appointments to government positions. The elite, along with the military, therefore, still controlled the machinery of government and, although a few liberals, such as Rui Barbosa, tried to persuade the government to introduce reforms in education and working conditions and pay and to consider the issue of land reform, nothing would really change until well into the next century.

In effect, of course, what had occurred was a military coup. The army ruled as a military dictatorship for the first five years following the coup in what was known as the 'Republic of the Sword'. Inevitably there were clashes between politicians and the newly politicised army officers, especially Deodoro who was authoritarian by nature. Eventually, in January 1891, the cabinet resigned. Meanwhile, the constitution demanded the election of the first president of the Republic who would serve until 1894. Deodoro was the obvious choice, but opponents to the military's involvement in government put forward a rival candidate, Prudente de Morais (1841–1902), president of the Constituent Assembly and a former governor of São Paulo. As anticipated, Deodoro won, by 129 votes to 97, and was sworn in as the first President of the Republic of Brazil on 26 February 1891. The margin of victory was sufficiently small to suggest that the new president was not the most popular of choices, but, as everyone was well aware, if he had lost, the army would almost certainly have stepped in and declared a dictatorship.

Deodoro took office amidst unrest, much of it caused by the economic crisis, the *Encilhamento*, a word borrowed from horse racing and suggestive of efforts to get rich quick. His handling of this situation was calamitous and gained him the animosity of Congress as did his lack of control over his ministries. Congress obstructed him at every opportunity. The Republicans from the South eventually withdrew their support from him and the provisional government. When the government was accused of corruption in November 1891, Deodoro dissolved the new National Congress, declaring a 'state of emergency' and assuming virtual dictatorial power, something for which he was heavily criticised and which lost him a great deal of support, even within the army. The vice president, Marshal Floriano Peixoto (1839–1895), conspired with other officers, leading to the seizure of warships in Guanabara Bay by Admiral Custódio José de Melo (1840–1902). De Melo threatened to open fire on Rio de Janeiro unless Deodoro recalled Congress. Deodoro responded by resigning on 23 November 1891 and Floriano, as Peixoto was popularly known, assumed the presidency, immediately recalling Congress.

The republic's second president – known as the 'Iron Marshal' – gained a reputation as an upholder of the constitution, but although he is said to have had a better understanding of ordinary people than his predecessor and succeeded in consolidating the republic, he was, in reality, not that different. He increasingly championed centralisation of power and nationalism but he faced stiff challenges. Some claimed that his presidency was unconstitutional because Deodoro had failed to serve the statutory two years in office and Floriano should, therefore, call a presidential election. His solution to this problem was simply to retain the title of 'Vice President'. He also faced opposition from senior officers of the Brazilian navy who resented the power and prestige of the army. Civil unrest raged in several states from the north to the south of the country and in 1893 revolutionaries occupied Santa Catarina and Paraná in Rio Grande do Sul, capturing the city of Curitiba. Ultimately, though, they were ill-equipped for outright war. In 1893, Admiral de Melo also acted against Floriano, once again threatening to bombard the capital, but the president refused to follow the example of Deodoro by resigning. By 1895, he had quashed the revolt in Rio Grande do Sul and had also succeeded in pacifying the naval rebels.

In March 1894, Floriano called a presidential election, following pressure from the Republicans running São Paulo who were providing vital financial, military and political support to him. They sought to safeguard national stability and unity and protect their state from an influx of foreign investment and immigrants. The *paulistas* had helped Floriano by founding the *Partido Republicano Federal* (Federal Republican Party) or PRF in 1893, but he was, of course, excluded by the constitution from standing for election for a second term. Now eager to replace military rule with a civilian leader from their own ranks, this coalition of senators and deputies from several states put forward Prudente de Morais Barros as their presidential candidate. This marked the end of political activity by the army for the time being and Floriano's subsequent death helped to further distance them from politics. The rival 1894 presidential candidate from Minas Gerais, Afonso Augusto Moreira Pena (1847–1909) lost heavily to Prudente – by 277,000 votes to 38,000 on 1 March 1894. It is worth noting, however, that with turmoil in Rio de Janeiro at the time, civil disorder in three of the country's southern states and the severely restricted nature of the franchise, only 2.2 per cent of the entire Brazilian population voted in this election.

The Rubber Boom 1879–1912

From the middle of the nineteenth century until the collapse of the market in 1910, rubber was vitally important to the Brazilian economy, bringing enormous profits to those involved in it. Natural rubber comes from a milky white fluid called latex drained from the *Hevea brasiliensis* tree found in abundance in the Brazilian state of Pará in the Amazon tropical rainforest. Latex, found in sap extracted from the tree trunk through a small hole bored in it, had been exploited by the native peoples for centuries, smoked over a fire and molded into objects. In the late eighteenth century, the colonial government was ordering boots made of latex from them but, until around 1830, no one viewed it as having any real commercial potential. Towards the end of that decade, however, British and North American scientists devised the process of vulcanisation, in which the raw sap could be stabilised by heating. Soon, rubber was being used in a variety of products such as tyres for bicycles and motorcars and electrical insulation devices. Demand went through the roof and before long entrepreneurs and immigrants were flooding into the Amazon region. These rubber tappers extracted the sap before forming it into large balls of rubber that were sold at local trading posts. It was then transported to the coast before shipping to foreign ports.

As a result of the boom in demand for rubber, a number of towns and cities grew astonishingly rapidly, populated by 'rubber barons' who had amassed great fortunes. One example was the Amazonian port city of Manaus which grew from just a few settlers to a bustling city of 100,000 by 1910. Its famous opera house was constructed in 1881 by a local politician, Antonio Jose Fernandes Júnior, who envisioned a 'jewel' in the heart of the Amazon rainforest. It was the second Brazilian city, after Campos dos Goytacazes in the state of Rio de Janeiro, to have electricity. Foreign capital was invested in the region to create trading houses and companies, amongst which was the one that built the Madeira-Mamoré railway, completed in 1912, which linked Brazil and Bolivia. 6,000 workers are said to have lost their lives during its construction.

By 1910, the Amazon's pre-eminence in the production of rubber was coming to an end. Several decades earlier, the Royal Botanical Gardens in Kew in England had smuggled some rubber seeds out of Brazil and produced trees in its hothouses in London. Seeds were then sent to the British colonies of Ceylon (modern-day Sri Lanka) and Malaya (modern-day Malaysia) where, unlike the Brazilian variety, they proved resistant to disease. They also produced a more abundant crop. The American Ford Motor Company tried to replicate what the British had done by creating rubber plantations at a place they called Fordlandia near the town of Santarém in Pará but the South American trees' lack of immunity to disease led to failure and the British, with their efficient and cost-effective Asian plantations, were left in control of the world's rubber market. The development of a synthetic substitute for natural rubber during World War One caused further damage to the Brazilian rubber industry. Only when the Allies were cut off from their Asian supplies during the Second World War did Amazonian rubber see a brief revival.

The *Paulista* and *Café-Com-Leite* Presidents

It could be said that the Brazilian First Republic was little more than a search for the best type of government to take the place of the monarchy, the argument alternating between centralisation and devolution of power to the states. The instability and factional violence of the 1890s was a result of the lack of agreement amongst the various elites about the most appropriate government model. The Constitution of 1891 had given the states considerable autonomy and, until the 1920s, the federal government was therefore dominated by a combination of the most powerful states in the Republic – Minas Gerais, Rio de Janeiro, Rio Grande do Sul and, of course, Sâo Paulo.

Prudente's first year in office saw the end of the Naval Revolt and the uprising in Rio Grande do Sul, although he was criticised for being too lenient to the Rio Grande do Sul rebels. In some quarters there was still a hankering for the monarchy and defenders of the Republic such as the ultra-national *Jacobins*, who had formed militia to defend Rio during the Naval Revolt, warned of monarchist conspiracies. Their warnings seemed to have been justified in 1896 as news reached the capital of a charismatic preacher, Antônio Vicente Mendes Maciel (1830–97), nicknamed *Conselheiro* who, in 1893, had assembled a community on an abandoned ranch at Canudos, a settlement 200 miles to the north of Salvador in Bahia. *Conselheiro* preached the return of the monarchy, describing the republicans as atheists. In 1896, he was engaged in a dispute with local officials over the cutting of timber that resulted in a force of police officers being sent to Canudos. They were sent packing, leading the Bahia Governor, Luís Viana (1846–1920), to request federal troops. Despite being armed with artillery and machine guns, they, too, were defeated and their commander was killed. The local dispute had quickly escalated into what became known as the *Guerra de Canudos* (War of Canudos), threatening the fledgling republic. There was protest and an outbreak of violence in Rio de Janeiro before an even larger military force was dispatched to the Northeast, consisting of 10,000 troops personally directed by the Minister of War, Marshal Carlos Machado Bittencourt (1840–97). During the ensuing siege, *Conselheiro* died, probably of dysentery, and Canudos was razed to the ground, more than half its 30,000 inhabitants being killed in the fighting and its aftermath. This 'monarchist threat' had been defeated but at a cost to the reputation and prestige of the army and of Prudente. The president's unpopularity was made clear when a young soldier, Marcelino Bispo (1875–98), tried to assassinate him on 5 November 1897. Bittencourt, the Minister of War, died after being stabbed protecting the president. When it emerged that Bispo had been encouraged in his assassination attempt by the editor of the *Jacobin* newspaper, *O Jacobino*, Prudente used the full force of the powers allocated to the presidency by the 1891 Constitution by coming down hard on Rio de Janeiro, especially the Military Club, a haunt of the *Jacobin* army officers, which was shut down.

The next president, Dr Manuel Ferraz de Campos Sales (1841–1913), governor of Sâo Paulo, was a *paulista*, like Prudente, emphasising the stranglehold that the political elite of the major states had on the country. To combat growing unrest in the states as well as factional fighting, Campos Sales devised a strategy known as the 'policy of the governors' by which a state's parliamentary delegates would be connected to the dominant political grouping in that state. As well as ending the factional fighting, he also hoped this would enhance the power of the executive branch of the government. He added to this by making the Chamber of Deputies more submissive to the executive. Unfortunately for him, it was only partially effective.

The 'policy of the governors' also proved useful in dealing with the Brazilian economy. Foreign debt inherited from the monarchy remained a huge problem and military expenditure during the 1890s did not help the situation. Between 1890 and 1897, the national debt increased by 30 per cent, resulting in even greater indebtedness to foreign banks. It was not helped by a fall in the price of coffee caused by abundant harvests in 1896 and 1897 that meant less foreign exchange coming into the country. Campos Sales arranged a funding loan that placed a great many difficult conditions on Brazil – all of its customs income from the port of Rio de Janeiro were to go to its creditors and further loans were prohibited until 1901. A programme of deflation also had to be undertaken. In an attempt to balance the books, Campos Sales increased federal taxes and introduced austerity measures, making his government very unpopular. By such desperate means, Brazil was prevented from going bankrupt, but the country would be hampered by these decisions for many years to come. Making all this happen required the support of the legislature and, as congressmen's loyalties lay with the political leader of their state and their parties, the president went directly to the state governors and the ruling elites. Campos Sales made a promise not to intervene in the states' internal affairs and the governors made it all work by using the *coronelismo* system. They provided positions and favours to the local *coronéis* who, in turn, delivered votes at the municipal and federal elections.

The governors had a vested interest in maintaining this system but that was dependent on the right man occupying the post of president. They met before each election, therefore, to select a suitable candidate and then ensured that he received enough votes. Naturally, the most powerful states, especially São Paulo and Minas Gerais, being the wealthiest and also possessing more citizens who satisfied the literacy requirement, were most influential in this process. Furthermore, their state political parties were far better organised than those of the other states. This way of manipulating the political machine came to be known as *café-com-leite* (coffee with milk) because of São Paulo's connection with the coffee industry and Minas Gerais' with milk. As a result, their candidates often achieved more than 90 per cent of the vote. This was helped by the fact that the ballot was rarely private and opposition was summarily dealt with. In this way, Brazil failed to develop a healthy multi-party political system. But the 'politics of the governors' undoubtedly had the desired effect, producing political stability and guaranteeing that the army would stay out of politics. As a system, however, it differed little from the corrupt political system that had prevailed during military rule and the Empire.

During his term of office Campos Sales succeeded in maintaining peace and order and in improving the nation's economic situation, but the austerity measures he had imposed on the Brazilian people led to a rise in the cost of living and made his government extremely unpopular. Nonetheless, the 'politics of the governors' managed to deliver a third *paulista* president in 1901 when Francisco de Paula Rodrigues Alves (1848–1919), governor of São Paulo, romped home in the presidential election by 592,000 votes to Quintino Bocaiúva's 43,000. Rodrigues Alves was chosen because it was expected that he would continue with the policies of Campos Sales. He had served as Minister of Finance in the governments of both Floriano and Prudente and had a reputation for financial expertise. He would also distinguish himself as a town planner, launching a major undertaking to modernise Rio de Janeiro.

Towards the end of his term of office, Rodrigues Alves proposed another São Paulo governor, Bernardino de Campos (1841–1915), as his successor but this time there was resistance from the smaller states. At the time, Rio Grande do Sul had been increasing in wealth and political status and one of its senators was the charismatic and powerful José Gomes Pinheiro Machado (1851–1915). For more than a decade, Pinheiro Machado, vice president of the senate, dominated Brazilian politics. He led a group of congressmen known as the *Bloco*, many of them from the less powerful northern and northeastern states, who gained a voice through his leadership. Machado became something of a 'kingmaker', as was proved in 1905 when he swung the votes of his bloc behind Afonso Pena, from Minas Gerais, former vice president to Rodrigues Alves. Afonso Pena won the election by 288,000 votes to a mere 5,000, bringing to an end the run of *paulista* presidents. When it came time to decide who would succeed him, Pinheiro Machado threw his voting bloc behind Marshal Hermes Rodrigues da Fonseca (1855–1923) – known as 'Hermes' – nephew of the Republic's first president, Deodoro. Incumbent President Pena chose as his nominee his finance minister, Davi Campista, another Minas Gerais politician whom the *paulista* elite believed would continue with the policies of Pena's government. Campista's candidacy came to an abrupt halt, however, with the death of Pena in June 1909. Vice President Nilo Procópio Peçanha (1867–1924) stepped into his shoes and then endorsed Hermes as presidential nominee for the 1910 election, to the dismay of the *paulistas*.

The election of 1910 was the first presidential election in the history of the *República Velha* that was not decided from the outset. The reason was the *paulistas'* choice of the noted liberal Brazilian statesman, Rui Barbosa, as a candidate to run against Hermes. After many years languishing in the political wilderness, the former Finance Minister had risen to national and international attention with his speeches in support of the rights of the world's smaller nations at the 1907 Hague Conference on International Peace where he had gained the nickname the 'Eagle of the Hague'. Barbosa railed against the corrupt oligarchies that had been running Brazil and he was also deeply concerned at Hermes' candidacy, seeing it as an attempt by the army to regain influence in government. He based his campaign on the simple choice between civilian rule and military rule, claiming that if the marshal won, Brazil would 'plunge forever into the servitude of the armed forces'. (Quoted in *Documentary History of Brazil*, E Bradford Burns, New York, Alfred A Knopf, 1967) The election was keenly fought, Rui Barbosa travelling widely to spread his ideas for liberal reform. Hermes' supporters were confident of victory, with only São

Paulo and Bahia lining up in favour of Barbosa. Army officers, concerned at Barbosa's anti-military stance, campaigned vigorously for Hermes and in the end he won 233,000 votes, while Rui only managed 126,000. The *paulistas* had been defeated in an election for the first time since 1894, even though the winning margin was the narrowest to date.

It seemed that every military president was blighted by a naval revolt and Hermes' version occurred in November 1910, just a few days after he had been sworn in as president. The mutiny on board two Brazilian battleships was soon quashed but it was evident that the relative peace of the last decade was at an end, a fact emphasised by a number of civil disturbances around the country. Being a military man, Hermes was more prepared to send in the troops than the civilian presidents before him, bringing rioters quickly under control.

He was determined to avenge himself on the members of the regional elites who had thrown their support behind Rui Barbosa in the 1910 election by replacing them with his own supporters. The army officers that he sent in to overthrow these regimes described their work as *política da salvacão* (politics of salvation) and there was a degree of irony in the fact that in rooting out Hermes' opponents, they were often also dealing with the reactionary elements Rui had criticised during his election campaign. There was serious fighting during this process, including the bombardment and invasion of Salvador.

By this time, Pinheiro Machado's *Partido Republicano Conservador* (Republican Conservative Party) or PRC, created to take the place of the *Bloco* in 1910, had begun to fall apart. He had also suffered during the period of the *política da salvacão* because many of his people were the very ones targeted by the army. Meanwhile, the *paulista* elite was determined to stop Pinheiro becoming president in 1914. When the oligarchs of Minas Gerais proposed their former governor Venceslau Brás (1868–1966), currently vice president, as a candidate, the *paulistas* immediately gave him their wholehearted support.

Realising all was lost Pinheiro gave Brás his support but ensured that his preferred candidate, the Maranhão senator Urbano Santos, was selected as vice-presidential candidate. Brás was elected with an overwhelming 90 per cent of the vote. Pinheiro's days as kingmaker were over and his brilliant political career was brought to an abrupt halt by his assassination in September 1915.

Brás's presidency was overshadowed by the outbreak of World War One. Brazil was initially reluctant to go to war. After all, there were large numbers of German immigrants in southern Brazil, many of whom were still loyal to their homeland. The Brazilian foreign minister, Lauro Müller, also had German antecedents. However, when Germany declared unrestricted submarine warfare in the Atlantic, Brazil, as an Atlantic trading nation, became involved. On 5 April 1917, the Brazilian ship *Parana* was sunk off the coast of France and three crew members lost their lives. When news of the sinking arrived in Brazil, riots broke out, an angry mob attacking German businesses in Rio de Janeiro. Brazil eventually declared war on 26 October, after the dismissal of Müller, Brazilian ships patrolling the South Atlantic and engaging in mine-sweeping off the coast of West Africa. An Expeditionary Force was being readied when the armistice was signed.

The 1918 election followed customary *café-com-leite* guidelines and former *paulista* president, Rodrigues Alves romped home with 99 per cent of the popular vote. However, illness prevented the newly elected president from taking office and he died the following year. It was decided to hold a special election but the decision as to who would replace Rodrigues Alves was a subject of debate between the elites of Minas Gerais and São Paulo. Eventually, Epitácio Pessôa (1865–1942), a Paraíba senator and Minister of Justice in the Campos Sales administration was selected. Pessôa was a delegate at the Versailles Peace Conference that followed the end of the First World War. In fact, he was still en route back to Brazil from the conference when the election was held. Once again, Rui Barbosa stood and once again, despite receiving almost 30 per cent of the vote, he was soundly beaten by the candidate of the elites, by 286,000 votes to 116,000.

Pessôa made enemies and antagonised the military as soon as he named his cabinet, appointing civilians to the ministries for war and the navy. By this time, Hermes, who had been living in Europe, had returned to Brazil where he was elected president of the Military Club in Rio de Janeiro. He became a major critic of Pessôa, especially when the new president vetoed the military budget. Pessôa faced still more criticism when it appeared that he was giving preferential treatment to his own home region of the Northeast by allocating 15 per cent of the federal budget to help install irrigation projects to deal with the drought there.

But Pessôa was no more than an interim president. For the 1922 election, the elites of São Paulo and Minas Gerais chose the Minas Gerais governor, Artur da Silva Bernardes (1875–1955). Once again, however, *café-com-leite* caused anger amongst the other states – Pernambuco, Rio de Janeiro and Rio Grande do Sul – who were never given a chance to nominate one of their own. They formed a coalition, the *Reação Republicana* (Republican Reaction) and threw their support behind Nilo Peçanha who had served briefly as president of Brazil from 1909 to 1910 following the death of President Afonso Pena. His campaign was based on claims that, under the *café-com-leite* system, the other states of Brazil suffered from neglect. Of course, there was little chance of defeating the 'official' candidate but some letters appeared in the *Correio da Manhã* newspaper that were purported to have been sent by Bernardes to a politician in Minas Gerais. They spoke disparagingly of Peçanha, describing him as a 'mulatto' and calling Hermes da Fonseca an 'overblown sergeant'. Corruption amongst army officers was also mentioned. Although the letters turned out to be forgeries, the army at the time accepted them as genuine and put all their support behind Bernardes' opponent Peçanha. In the closest election in the history of the republic, Bernardes scraped in with 56 per cent of the popular vote. The elite had won again.

The disgruntled military now acted against the wishes of the presidency. It had been Pessôa's habit to order the army in where there were problems with state elections, which Hermes believed was an abuse of power, using the army for political ends. He sent a telegram to the commander of the garrison at Recife suggesting that he resist any presidential directive to intervene in situations involving local politics. When he was informed of this, Pessôa was furious, immediately placing Hermes under house arrest and shutting down the Military Club for six months. A couple of days later there was a mutiny at Fort Copacabana in Rio de Janeiro that its participants said was aimed at 'rescuing the army's honour'. Government forces besieged the fort and bombarded it by sea and by air. The following day, most of the mutineers surrendered but a group of eighteen had resolved to fight to the death. They made their last stand on the beach where sixteen of them were killed. Afterwards, a state of emergency was declared, hundreds of cadets were expelled from the army school and officers who had participated in the mutiny were posted to remote garrisons.

The 1922 Revolt was the foundation for a movement involving junior officers of the Brazilian army that became known as *tenentismo* as most of those involved were lieutenants (*tenentes*). They believed that the Republic would never achieve its full potential as a nation under civilian government and demanded radical reform, both economically and socially to alleviate poverty in Brazil. At the same time, however, the *tenentes* realised that there was little hope of bringing down the regional oligarchies and party bosses without the use of force and without that their movement never really progressed into a full-blown political entity. Brazilian politics continued as before.

As Bernardes took office, Brazil was in a parlous state,

embroiled in both economic and political crises. He added to the problems by intervening in state politics – claiming he was merely trying to maintain law and order – and often installing his own men where he could. He took his revenge on the press by introducing censorship and refused to grant an amnesty to those involved in the 1922 revolt. He courted even greater unpopularity with a strict, conservative fiscal policy, demonstrated most vividly in his withdrawal of financial support for the valorisation – manipulation of the price – of coffee. He also withdrew funding for the irrigation projects that Pessôa had launched during his term of office. So unpopular did Bernardes become that he rarely left the presidential palace.

Finally, he faced a major crisis with what is called the 'second Fifth of July'. On that date, two years to the day after the revolt of 1922, there was a better prepared uprising of young officers in São Paulo with the aim of bringing down the Bernardes government. The leader was a retired Rio Grande do Sul officer, General Isidoro Dias Lopes (1865–1949) and amongst other prominent military figures involved were Eduardo Gomes (1896–1981), Newton Estillac Leal (1893–1955), João Cabanas (1895–1974) and Miguel Costa (1885–1959), the latter an important officer in the São Paulo *Força Pública* (State Militia). They demanded the restoration of constitutional liberties and denounced what they described as Bernardes' excessive use of presidential authority. They succeeded in taking control of the city for twenty-two days until they were forced to withdraw. Other rebellions erupted in Sergipe, Amazonas and Rio Grande do Sul. The São Paulo rebels left the city and headed west, establishing their base in western Paraná and awaiting another force, led by Captain Luís Carlos Prestes (1898–1990), that was marching north from Rio Grande do Sul. The two groups joined up and marched into the interior of the country, hoping to persuade the peasants to join with them in bringing Bernardes down. For two years the *Coluna Prestes* (Prestes Column), as they had come to be known, marched across the North and

Northeast, fighting several battles en route to Bolivia where they arrived and finally disbanded in 1927. The 'Prestes Column' failed in its principal aim of bringing down the government but it gained a huge amount of publicity and helped to make people aware of rural poverty. Prestes became a Marxist in 1929, visited the Soviet Union in 1931 and, in 1943, after a number of years in prison, became leader of the Brazilian Communist Party. *Tenentismo* carried on, seeking economic development as a way to create social and political change in Brazil.

Café-com-leite continued unrelentingly and, in 1926, it was the turn of the *paulistas* to come up with a candidate. After all, the last *paulista* president, Rodrigues Alves, although elected in 1918, had fallen sick before taking office which meant the last *paulista* actually to serve as president had been the same politician during his first stint from 1902 to 1906. Washington Luís (1869–1957), governor of São Paulo, was duly nominated by a meeting of state governors, with Fernando de Melo Viana (1878–1954) of Minas Gerais as his vice-presidential candidate. With Rui Barbosa now dead, there was little opposition and it was an election marked by general apathy. Needless to say, Washington Luís won 98 per cent of the vote.

One of the new president's cabinet appointments had immense importance for the future of Brazil – that of Getúlio Dornelles Vargas (1882–1954) as Minister of Finance. The forty-three-year-old politician from Rio Grande do Sul would become one of the most significant figures in Brazilian history.

6

The Vargas Era
1930 to 1954

Population and Industry in the Nineteen-Thirties

Between 1920 and 1940, Brazil's population increased by slightly more than 25 per cent, from 30,600,000 to 41,100,000. It was a youthful population, too, 54 per cent being under the age of twenty. Foreign immigration fell between 1920 and 1940 as a result of both the Depression and a 1934 Constitution that limited the number of immigrants. There had also been internal movement. Following the collapse of the rubber market in 1910, around 14 per cent of the population of the North moved out. Meanwhile, the South and Centre-South enjoyed a population growth of 11.7 per cent as a result of such internal movement.

Around 1930, the coffee industry entered a crisis and coffee's role in agriculture seriously declined with cotton becoming increasingly important both for export and for domestic use. In the late 1920s, coffee represented 71 per cent of Brazilian exports; by 1939, it had fallen to 41.7 per cent while cotton rose from 2.1 per cent to 18.6 per cent. Industry was on the rise. In 1920, agriculture was responsible for 79 per cent of the gross national product, but by 1920 this figure had declined to 57 per cent. Industry grew rapidly between 1933 and 1939, even though the government contributed little to this growth. Unfortunately, the upheaval caused to trade by the Second World War put paid to Brazil's industrial momentum.

The Revolution of 1930

At the start of 1929, as his term of office drew to a close, President Washington Luís surprised everyone by nominating a fellow *paulista* as presidential candidate, the Conservative governor of São Paulo, Júlio Prestes (1882–1946). This alienated the politicians of Minas Gerais who allied themselves with those of Rio Grande do Sul. They were joined by other disaffected politicians in the *Alianca Liberal* (Liberal Alliance) to agree on the nomination of Getúlio Vargas as their candidate in the forthcoming election. João Pessôa (1878–1930), governor of the Northeastern state of Paraíba and nephew of former president Epitácio Pessôa was nominated as his vice-presidential running mate. This helped to bring the sugar barons of the Northeast into the Liberal Alliance. They already had numerous grievances against the *paulista* coffee oligarchs amongst which was the termination of irrigation projects in the drought-stricken Northeast.

Getúlio Vargas was from a wealthy family of Azorean Portuguese descent and had a military career before studying law. Having already been elected to the Rio Grande do Sul state legislature, in 1922 he entered the Chamber of Deputies, becoming the leader of his state's congressional delegation. Eventually, in 1926, he was appointed Finance Minister by Washington Luís but resigned in 1928 to be elected governor of his home state. In that position, he began to rise to national prominence, especially through his campaigning for the end of electoral corruption and for the introduction of universal suffrage and secret ballots. Vargas had been a populist governor with a vision for change in Brazilian politics, an economic nationalist who supported industrial development and liberal reforms. This was very much against the aims of the *paulista* coffee oligarchy and the landed elites who had no interest in Brazilian industry.

The election of 1930 took place against the unsettled

backdrop of the Great Depression which hit Brazilians hard, especially those engaged in coffee production. In the two years after the United States stock market crash of 29 October 1929, the price of a pound of coffee plummeted from 22.5 cents to just 8 cents, leading to a catastrophic drop in foreign exchange earnings. The valorisation programme, introduced to safeguard the price of coffee, collapsed, weakening the central government that depended for support on the wealthy coffee elite. Gold reserves were depleted and the exchange rate fell dramatically. A dire crisis developed with coffee producers' warehouses full of a harvest that they could not sell and the government facing a desperate balance of payments crisis. The popularity of Washington Luís's government was at an all-time low with every section of Brazilian society.

On 1 March 1930 Júlio Prestes secured the presidency by a narrow margin in an election in which fraud was rife. The younger members of the opposition were very unhappy with the result and allied with rebels in the military. On 3 October, a revolution was launched in Minas Gerais and Rio Grande do Sul, erupting in the Northeast the following day. Several weeks later, on 24 October, just three weeks before Prestes' inauguration, as rebel forces prepared to invade the state of São Paulo for what would almost certainly be the most important confrontation of the conflict, members of the military high command overthrew the government in Rio de Janeiro. General Augusto Fragoso (1869–1945), Admiral Isaías de Noronha (1874–1963) and General Mena Barreto (1874–1933) formed a junta, but it did not remain in power for long. They quickly yielded to popular demonstrations and demands from their troops for Getúlio Vargas to be allowed to assume the presidency. Vargas, meanwhile, was travelling by train from the South to São Paulo and onward to the capital where he was triumphantly welcomed by 3,000 Rio Grande do Sul troops. Brazil's First Republic came to an end when Vargas became president on 3 November 1930.

Initially, he was heavily influenced by the *tenentes* who insisted on a complete re-structuring of Brazil in every sphere – political, social and economic. Eager to establish a modern state they also wanted to provide help in the form of social and economic reform for the poor people of the interior. They had long argued against the state oligarchies and advocated a centralised, authoritarian government. Their influence weakened in 1932, however, due to their radical and poorly received performances as state *interventores*, a role that the new president introduced to replace state governors.

Vargas immediately set about consolidating the rule of his provisional government by dissolving all federal, state and municipal legislative bodies and himself assuming executive and legislative power. He declared he would govern as a dictator, ruling by decree. No end date was provided for his term of office but he would ultimately rule Brazil for fifteen years.

The traditional oligarchies were replaced by military men, technocrats and keen young politicians. The state was centralised and it promoted industrialisation, providing protection for urban workers. The armed forces were encouraged to play an important role in government and to ensure stability. The *Código dos Interventores* of August 1931 dealt with the appointment of the military men who replaced the governors and set limits on states' independence. They were banned from acting autonomously in fiscal matters, were no longer permitted to raise foreign loans without the permission of the central government and spending on military police forces was limited.

The Church played a vital role in ensuring support for Vargas, a relationship embodied in the unveiling of the famous statue of *Cristo Redentor* (Christ the Redeemer) on Corcovado Mountain in Rio de Janeiro in 1931 to commemorate the day Columbus discovered America. The government passed legislation in the Church's favour and the Church ensured that its members supported Vargas.

Coffee production remained a problem, of course, and the Vargas government dealt with it by forming the *Departamento Nacional do Café* or DNC which guaranteed that the government would use a percentage of its export receipts to purchase existing and future stocks of coffee. It was a scheme that would remain in place until 1944 in which time more than 78 million sacks of coffee beans were destroyed – equivalent to three years' global coffee consumption. The economic situation remained perilous, however, and in September 1931 repayment of foreign debts was suspended.

There was opposition to Vargas, especially from the *paulistas* who had been removed from their prestigious positions. They were especially upset when Lieutenant João Alberto, a *tenente* from the Northeast, was appointed *interventor* for their state. They declared him to be a Communist after he increased the wages of factory workers and gave land to people who had supported the 1930 Revolution. Eventually, on 9 July 1932, the resentment in São Paulo spilled over into an uprising known as the 'Constitutionalist Revolution' or the 'Paulista War'. But poor organisation and a lack of preparation doomed the revolt to failure, the rebels finally surrendering on 9 September. The rest of the country considered the *paulistas* to have displayed disloyalty to the state and their reputation was severely damaged by their actions.

Vargas's labour policy was clear from the beginning. He sought to prevent the working class from organising themselves into a coherent opposition force but at the same time wanted to encourage them to become supporters of his government. To this end, he immediately clamped down on left-wing political parties and unions. The Brazilian Communist Party (*Partido Comunista do Brasil*) or PCB was hit especially hard. To deal with the working class, the Ministry of Labour, Industry, and Commerce was created and to deal with the unions, new laws were introduced that meant unions were, effectively, taken over by the government and could do nothing without ministerial approval. Workers were protected by departments such as the *Juntas de Conciliação e Julgamento* (Bureaux of Reconciliation and Arbitration) that provided mediation in disputes between bosses and employees.

There had already been attempts to improve education in the 1920s, but Vargas's administration set about reforms immediately and established a Ministry of Education and Health. Until then, secondary education had been little more than preparation for entry into university. Now, the aim was to operate a curriculum focused on a high school diploma that was necessary to gain admittance to university.

Creating the *Estado Nôvo*

Vargas had described his regime as 'provisional' and in February 1932 promised to 'reconstitutionalise' Brazil. A year later, therefore, a Constituent Assembly was elected with the aim of drafting and passing a new constitution as well as electing a new president. The first of these aims – the new constitution – was achieved on 16 July 1934, effectively bringing Vargas's provisional government to an end. The 1934 Constitution was, in actual fact, little more than the 1891 Constitution with the addition of decrees that had been passed since 1930. The secret ballot was added as was the extension of the franchise to eighteen-year-olds and to women in employment. The National Congress with its two houses was re-introduced and a new provision was made for 50 appointed 'class representatives' to join the 300 elected deputies. This anti-democratic move demonstrated little faith in the electoral system but, on the other hand, the constitution did make provisions for the direct election of the president for the first time, with the proviso that the first president would be chosen by the Constituent Assembly. Inevitably, Getúlio Vargas was chosen by the assembly as the first president, to serve a term of four years although ineligible to succeed himself, as laid down in the Constitution. His token opponent in the election was Borges de Medeiros (1863–1961), the former governor of Rio Grande do Sul who lost by 175 votes to 59. Elections to the state legislatures were held in October 1934.

Constitutional government brought a two-party political system to Brazil for the first time. The left was represented by the PCB which had gained ground due to the global depression that was playing havoc with the Brazilian economy as it was with every other nation. The PCB's leader was Luís Carlos Prestes who had so gallantly led the 'Prestes Column' in 1924. Prestes had turned to Marxism while exiled in Buenos Aires and in 1935 returned clandestinely to Brazil where he remained in hiding while leading the opposition to Vargas, calling for a socialist revolution to overthrow the government. The PCB was at the forefront of an alliance of left-wing organisations known as the *Aliança Nacional Libertadora* (National Liberation Alliance) or ANL, that published a programme consisting of five points – suspension of the payment of Brazil's foreign debt; the nationalisation of all foreign businesses in Brazil; agrarian reform; a guarantee of individual rights; and the creation of a government in which anyone could participate, 'according to his abilities'. Opposing the ANL was the nationalist AIB, the *Acão Integralista Brasileira* (Brazilian Integralist Movement) that had been formed in São Paulo in 1932 in imitation of the fascist parties that had come to prominence in Europe. Led by a journalist, Plínio Salgado (1895–1975), the members of the AIB wore a uniform of green shirts bearing the sigma symbol (Σ) and jackboots while campaigning for an 'integral' state with an authoritarian leader. They blamed liberalism, socialism and capitalism (controlled, they claimed, by the Jews) for all of the world's problems. 'God, Country and Family' was their watchword, trumpeted at massive rallies that often resulted in violence with members of the ANL. During its heyday, the

AIB's membership is estimated to have been between 100,000 and 200,000, a significant number, given Brazilians' general lack of political involvement.

Vargas had supporters amongst the army. By the end of 1933, 36 of the 40 generals in the military owed their positions to the Vargas administration, providing him with a loyal core within the armed forces. Unlike the fascist leaders in Europe at the time, however, he refused to use his position to create an organised political movement espousing his particular political ideology. Rather, he chose to remain aloof from factions and parties. His natural inclination was, of course, to support the Integralists and oppose Communism and he was concerned at the increasingly militant direction in which the ANL was being taken. Furthermore, during 1934, Brazil was plagued by middle-class unrest and strikes in Rio de Janeiro, São Paulo and Rio Grande do Norte, throwing transport, communications and banking into chaos. In response, in early 1935, the president welcomed the introduction of a Law of National Security that, amongst other things, prohibited civil servants from striking and banned anti-government propaganda and the creation of organisations or political parties that aimed to illegally subvert political or social order. His fears were well grounded because, in November 1935, there were rebellions by pro-Communist army officers in several cities. These uprisings, however, were occasioned more by gripes about pay and conditions than by revolutionary fervour and were soon suppressed, but not before the deaths of several officers. Such incidents gave Vargas the opportunity to suppress the Communists and others on the Left and, with the wholehearted support of the Church, the army and the middle class, he suspended the 1934 Constitution, reasserted autocratic rule and introduced the *Commisão National de Repressão ao Communismo* (National Commission for Stopping Communism). Communist party offices were raided, files seized and several thousand members of the PCB were imprisoned or deported. Amongst those arrested was Luís Carlos Prestes who was sentenced to sixteen years in prison. The *Tribunal de Segurança Nacional* (National Security Council) was launched initially to investigate people involved in the 1935 rebellion. It actually remained in session for ten years. The country was declared to be in 'a state of war' for ninety days, a status that was renewed constantly until June 1937 when Vargas declared the *Estado Nôvo* (New State). It would last until 1945.

Elections were due to be held in January 1938 and candidates began to jockey for position in the eighteen months prior to that date. Vargas was, of course, barred by the constitution from standing which meant that other political figures began to emerge, such as the apparent favourite, Armando de Sales Oliveira, governor of São Paulo. He campaigned as a liberal constitutionalist with the support of the *Partido Constitucionalista* (Constitutionalist Party) aiming to devolve power to the states once more. The government put forward the Minister for Transport and Public Works, José Américo de Almeida (1887–1980), a politician from the Northeast who enjoyed the not inconsiderable support of his home region, Minas Gerais and the Vargas-supporting areas of São Paulo and Rio Grande do Sul. He described himself as the 'People's Candidate'. Meanwhile, representing the Integralists was the party's leader, Plínio Salgado.

As campaigning progressed, repressive measures began to be lifted and three hundred people were released from prison. Vargas, meanwhile, was convinced that he should remain in power, fearing for Brazilian economic and social development if he were to go. His strategy became known as *continuismo* (continuism) and to implement it, he plotted with his senior generals to create internal unrest and instability, the perfect conditions for a coup. The military were only too happy to support him because his rule had been beneficial to them. He had doubled the size of the army for instance, from 38,000 in 1927 to 75,000 ten years later. The vehicle for their actions was a document known as the 'Cohen Plan' that was a little too conveniently discovered by army officers in Rio de Janeiro. It described plans for a Communist uprising in which leading members of the government would be assassinated. Vargas disclosed its contents in a national radio broadcast at the end of September 1937, frightening Congress so much that its members voted to reintroduce the state of war and to suspend the constitution for ninety days. On 10 November, with rumours of a military coup mounting, troops surrounded the National Congress building. Vargas declared a state of national emergency to protect the nation from dangers that he blamed on the presidential campaign. He claimed to be saving Brazil from civil war and announced the enactment of a new constitutional charter written by Francisco Campos (1891–1968), a Minas Gerais lawyer. The 1937 Constitution did not undergo any kind of approval process, but was, rather, imposed upon Brazil by Vargas to whom it gave what amounted to dictatorial powers. The power of the judicial branch of government was suppressed, as was the autonomy of the states that were to be governed by federal officials who would wield both legislative and executive powers. The presidential term of office was extended to six years, securing Vargas's leadership until 1943. The general tenor of the document borrowed much from European fascism, the antithesis of the liberal constitutionalism present in the Constitution of 1934. Congress was dissolved, the press was censored and all political parties were banned, even the fascistic AIB, although the Integralists were gratified by the adoption of what they claimed to be their philosophy. There was little resistance, the Communists and the leftist *Aliança Nacional Libertadora* having already been dealt with. The Intergralists, however, were dismayed when their leader Salgado was not appointed to the Ministry of Education, as had been anticipated, and vented their frustration by launching an attack on the presidential palace. Armed with guns, Vargas and his daughter, Alzira, are said to have fought them off, leading to their subsequent acclamation as heroes. The inept nature of the assault gave rise to suspicions that it had actually been concocted by pro-government elements in order to give the president an excuse to suppress the AIB which he did ruthlessly. Salgado fled to Portugal where he remained until 1945.

Vargas now began to portray himself as the guardian of the workers. From 1939, he staged May Day celebrations in football stadiums, launching his speeches with the words 'Workers of Brazil...' and always using the occasion to announce a measure with social implications guaranteed to delight the assembled crowds. He also made effective use of the media, striving to create an image of him as a friend and father of the Brazilian people. Eventually, the government set up a propaganda ministry, the *Departamento de Imprensa e Propaganda* (Department of Press and Propaganda) or DIP, under the direct control of the president. This office kept a close watch over films, the press, radio, theatre and literature, prohibiting the entry into the country of material that 'might harm Brazil's interests', as they put it. The daily radio show, *Hora do Brasil*, trumpeting government initiatives and successes, was broadcast by the DIP.

During the *Estado Nôvo*, torture and imprisonment without trial became the norm. Vargas justified it by declaring that Brazil was, effectively, in a state of war. He made frequent use of the term 'national reconstruction' and appealed to the nationalist tendencies of the Brazilian military and middle classes by promoting the notion of the 'corporate state' that he claimed would benefit everyone, that would not only bring prosperity to the nation but also deliver an independent economy – achieved through a programme of industrialisation – and military strength. Corporatism also implied that there should be a great deal of federal involvement – both in terms of planning and investment – in developing the country, embodied in projects such as the 'march to the west' by which the federal government helped migrants to settle and developed Brazil's underpopulated western regions. The corporate state also embraced various bodies and organisations such as trade unions for skilled workers, the Ministry of Labour being given power over the appointment of officials and authority to establish tribunals to arbitrate in disputes between the unions and the employers.

Vargas's good relations with the army were shaped by shared goals. Like them, of course, he favoured modernisation through autocratic rule. There were still divided opinions amongst military ranks about matters such as foreign policy or economic development, which gave Vargas scope for manipulation.

As for the Brazilian economy during the *Estado Nôvo*, there were efforts to establish industry sufficient to replace imports with products produced domestically. This was made even more crucial as the Second World War became increasingly inevitable, bringing the prospect of restrictions on trade. There were nationalist elements to the way in which the economy was allowed to work. For instance, the exploitation of minerals was restricted to Brazilians and only insurance companies and banks whose shareholders were Brazilian were allowed to do business. Foreign companies had to become Brazilian within a set period of time.

The Second World War and the Fall of Vargas

Entering the Second World War on the side of the Allies, Brazil was the only Latin American country to take an active combat role in Europe. Until 1941, Vargas had insisted on neutrality but an agreement was devised by his foreign minister, Osvaldo Aranha (1894–1960), whereby each of the nations of the American continent agreed to align with any other country of the continent attacked by an external power. When the Japanese attacked the United States naval base at Pearl Harbor on 7 December 1941, therefore, Brazil's entry into the war became a foregone conclusion. Vargas used the opportunity to bolster his prestige, appealing to Brazilian patriotism. His reputation benefited from the exploits of the *Força*

Expedicionária Brasileira (Brazilian Expeditionary Force), about 25,700 Brazilian troops who saw combat in Italy. They had been dispatched on his own personal orders, in opposition to the advice of some of his senior generals. There was a very evident contradiction, however, in Vargas's support of those who sought to liberate people from repressive and authoritarian regimes in Europe while himself heading such a government. A manifesto symptomatic of this underlying criticism of the president was published in Minas Gerais in October 1943. Signed by ninety prominent citizens of the state it called for the nation to rise up in support of the restoration of liberal constitutionalism. 'If we fight against fascism at the side of the United Nations so that liberty and democracy may be restored to all people,' it said, 'certainly we are not asking too much in demanding for ourselves such rights and guarantees.' (Quoted in *A History of Brazil* by E. Bradford Burns, Columbia University Press, New York, 1993) Naturally, Vargas used the fact that the country was at war to denounce the manifesto as unpatriotic. It was an excuse to which he also turned to cancel the presidential election of 1943, claiming that it would be delayed until after the conclusion of the war.

As an Allied victory became increasingly certain, there was growing pressure not only in Brazil for an end to autocratic, dictatorial rule; throughout Latin America people were agitating for democracy. Even the Brazilian military who had developed an appreciation of American democracy while working with their US equivalents during the war began to lean towards a more open political system. It was made known to Vargas that the period of autocratic rule would have to come to an end. No fool, Vargas had already seen the writing on the wall for dictatorship and had been preparing for the approaching election. He began to emphasise his populist credentials, fostering a close relationship with the trade unions, asserting his 'man of the people' status to the Brazilian working class and reminding them how his *Estado Nôvo* had given them a minimum wage, better pensions and better healthcare. There was opposition, however. Students had started to demonstrate against the Vargas leadership in 1943, founding the *União Nacional dos Estudiantes* or UNE (National Union of Students) and marching with their mouths gagged in protest at the lack of freedom of speech. The march ended in the deaths of two demonstrators at the hands of the police.

A major factor in the fall of Vargas was the withdrawal of support for the *Estado Nôvo* by General Pedro de Góis Monteiro (1889–1956). He had been one of Vargas's military supporters and was the 'discoverer' of the Cohen Plan documents, but by 1945 he was convinced that politics must change in Brazil. He had been ambassador to the Emergency Committee for the Political Defense of Latin America, based in Montevideo, Uruguay, but resigned that position to return home to work at the Ministry of War and, effectively, oversee the conclusion of the Vargas Era.

In February 1945 an extraordinary interview appeared in the press. In it, 1938 presidential candidate, José Américo de Almeida, demanded that an election be held soon and that Getúlio Vargas should be prohibited from standing. What was extraordinary was that such an article had not been censored, a sure sign that things were changing. Of course, due to the repression of recent years, there were no real opposition candidates to Vargas, and the best bet seemed to be a military candidate. In March 1945, therefore, air force Brigadier Eduardo Gomes announced his candidacy. His participation in the 1922 *tenentes* revolt made him a particular favourite of junior military officers but, because he had been critical of the 1937 coup, he also enjoyed support from opponents of Vargas. Vargas made an amendment to the constitution, declaring that there would be elections for the presidency as well as for Congress and state legislatures. After initially appearing to be keen to stand for president, in a speech in March 1945, he finally acceded to demands that he withdraw, announcing his retirement from politics. The 'official' candidate chosen to succeed him was his Minister of War, General Eurico Gaspar Dutra (1883–1974), born in Mato Grasso, who had opposed alignment with the Allies during the war. A couple of political parties emerged. Supporting Dutra was the *Partido Social Democrático* (Social Democratic Party) or PSD and on the side of Gomes was the *Uniao Democrático Nacional* (National Democratic Union) or UDN.

Although he had claimed to have retired, suspicions of Vargas's intentions remained. When a new political party, *Partido Trabalhista Brasileiro* or PTB (Brazilian Labour Party) was founded, naming him as honorary president, some wondered if he might be on the verge of attempting a coup. The *Queremistas*, a group of his supporters, coined the slogan '*Queremos Getúlio*' ('We want Getúlio') and campaigned for the cancellation of the presidential election, leaving only a constitutional assembly to be elected. Until that assembly had devised a new constitution, they insisted, Vargas would remain president. None of these initiatives worked in Vargas's favour, however, and as both candidates in the election were military men, they were not so easily dispensed with as the civilian candidates of 1937. Furthermore, the military was unhappy with Vargas by this time, especially after he had re-established diplomatic relations with the Soviet Union, freed Communist prisoners and had legalised the Brazilian Communist Party. They had learned from their neighbour, Argentina, where, as they saw it, the country's leader, Juan Perón (1895–1974), had returned to power on a tide of populism while the military had stood and watched. The Brazilian army acted quickly, surrounding the presidential palace on 29 October 1945 and demanding Vargas's resignation. The president quickly realised there was little point in resistance; he resigned and travelled to his ranch in Rio Grande do Sul. Getúlio Vargas exited the political scene, but it would not be the last that Brazil would see of him.

1945 – the Changing of the Guard

The military and the liberal opposition put in place a caretaker government headed by José Linhares (1886–1957), the Brazilian Chief Justice and presidential and congressional elections were scheduled for 2 December 1945, while elections for the state legislatures were slated for the following year. As the two candidates campaigned Gomes appeared to have the upper hand, if the number of people attending his rallies was anything to go by. Dutra's campaigning was unexceptional while Gomes championed the urban middle class who longed for economic liberalism and democracy. Vargas maintained his distance but a week prior to the election he came out in favour of Dutra, qualifying his support with the statement: 'I shall be at the people's side against the President if the candidate's promises are not fulfilled'. Finally, on election-day, the Brazilian people demonstrated their enthusiasm for the democratic process by turning out in huge numbers. The 1930 presidential election had been decided by 900,000 people. By 1945, with urban workers enfranchised for the first time, the percentage of the population entitled to vote rose from 5.7 per cent of the population to 13.4 per cent. 6,200,000 people voted, a turnout of 83.1 per cent. The fact that the ballot was secret reduced intimidation and coercion by the state political machines and the landed elite and encouraged many to vote.

Despite his unimpressive campaign, Dutra won a resounding victory, polling 3,251,507 votes to Gomes' 2,039,341 – 55.4 per cent to 34.7 per cent. Interestingly, an anti-militarist independent candidate, the former mayor of Petrópolis, Yedo Fiúza (1894–1975), who was backed by the Brazilian Communist Party, took an impressive 10 per cent of the vote. Vargas, nominated by the PSB and his Brazilian Labour Party in various states, was elected senator for Rio Grande do Sul and deputy in six states as well as Rio de Janeiro. He opted to serve as senator for Rio Grande do Sul. It was a good election for the Social

Democratic Party which emerged with 151 deputies and 26 senators, giving it a decent majority in both houses of Congress. The National Democratic Union, meanwhile, had only 77 deputies and 10 senators, its poor performance ascribed to the removal of Vargas from office, eliminating the principal focus of their criticism. The Brazilian Labour Party had a disappointing election, gaining just 22 deputies and 2 senators. The Communist Party, on the other hand, had every right to be pleased with its performance. Fourteen Communist deputies were elected and its leader, Luís Carlos Prestes, fresh out of prison, but still the most famous politician in Brazil after Vargas, was elected to represent the Federal District in the Senate.

The Administration of Eurico Gaspar Dutra (1946 to 1951)

The most pressing task for the new government was the drafting of a new constitution, devised by the Chamber of Deputies and the Senate. The 1946 Constitution was the first Brazilian constitution to provide full political freedom. Even the Brazilian Communist Party was made legal, although it did not retain that status for long. It was the last constitution officially to use the name *Estados Unidos do Brazil*. In it, Brazil was defined as a federal republic with a presidential style of government; the president's term of office was fixed at five years, the incumbent could not succeed himself and the role of vice president was reinstated; there were greater limitations on presidential power, but the role retained powers of intervention in affairs of state; the power of the National Congress was restored but the franchise remained limited to those of both sexes, aged eighteen or more, who were literate; and the vote was denied to members of the army, navy and air force. Workers' rights were left largely unchanged from the *Estado Nôvo* but a list of 'essential' occupations that were banned from striking included just about every conceivable job.

The Communist Party, as demonstrated by its performance in the election, enjoyed great popularity at the time and it is estimated that it had around 200,000 members. But as the Communist threat to the balance of power began to emerge in civil wars in Greece and China and with the first stirrings of the Cold War, attitudes began to change. There was undoubtedly pressure from the American government for something to be done to halt its growing popularity in Brazil and this, coupled with the senior military's traditional hatred of it, persuaded the government once again to outlaw the Communist Party. The law was passed in January 1948 and all Communist deputies, senators and councillors were removed from office. Admittedly, the action was nowhere near as draconian as it had been a decade earlier, but the PCB would never regain the influence that it enjoyed between 1945 and 1947. Repression returned to Brazil as unions opposed to government policies were closed down or taken over.

Dutra turned out to be just as uninspiring a leader as he had been a campaigner and suppressing Communism was about the only decisive thing he achieved during his presidency. His administration pursued a liberal economic policy. In fact, the Brazilian economy was in a good state as substantial foreign funds had been accumulated from exports during the war. These were soon wiped out, however, as imports flooded the country, encouraged by a favourable exchange rate. In response, in 1947, restrictions were placed on the import of consumer goods while still permitting essential imports such as industrial equipment and fuel. Towards the end of Dutra's regime, there were signs of economic growth, but while the cost of living increased rapidly, wages were going down, mainly because the trade unions were unable to fight on behalf of their members due to the repression of their activities.

The Return of Getúlio Vargas

The politics of personality were still strong in Brazil, despite the emergence of new political parties, and no political personality loomed larger than that of Getúlio Vargas. He was a senator, although his appearances in the Senate were rare. There was a great deal of speculation about his political intentions and there was little doubt that he still wielded enormous influence, retaining the support of many Brazilians as a result of benefits derived from the *Estado Nôvo*. He devised a new political philosophy – *trabalhismo* (labourism) – that he expounded in a series of speeches, building a solid core of support around the country, playing particularly on the image of himself as 'father of the poor'. Populism was one thing, but to achieve political success in Brazil, it was still necessary to build relationships with vested interests, especially the military. With this in mind, he obtained a guarantee from Góis Monteiro that the armed forces would not stand in his way if he were to be elected president.

He became the nominee of the PTB whilst maintaining good relations with the PSB and the *Partido Social Progressista* (Progressive Socialist Party) or PSP, led by Adhemar de Barros (1901–69), the increasingly popular governor of São Paulo. Barros was liked by the working class of both São Paulo and Rio de Janeiro and his favouring of Vargas would be vital in returning the former dictator to power. The incumbent Dutra, on the other hand, withheld his support from Vargas because he received no guarantee that he would perpetuate his policies. Instead, he persuaded the PSD to nominate the virtually unknown Minas Gerais politician, Christiano Monteiro Machado (1893–1953) who had little chance of success as the party's support for him was weak and he failed to venture outside his home state throughout the entire campaign. Eduardo Gomes was again nominated by the UDN but his campaign was hopelessly out of touch to the extent that he advocated repealing the minimum wage law, hardly a vote-winner. Vargas criticised the conservative nature of Dutra's administration and promised, if elected, to provide federal aid to industry as well as to increase wages. He unashamedly embraced populism, stating in one celebrated speech in Rio de Janeiro: 'If I am elected on 3 October, as I take office the people will climb the steps of Catete with me. And they will remain with me in power'. (*Politics in Brazil 1930–1964: An Experiment in Democracy*, Thomas E Skidmore, New York, Oxford University Press, 2007) There was a record turnout on election day, with more than 8 million votes recorded. Vargas won with 3.8 million – 48.7 per cent of the vote; Gomes was second with 2.3 million votes; and third was Machado with 1.7 million.

This time it would have to be different. Vargas had been elected in a democratic process and could no longer act as a dictator. He would have to work with the National Congress to enact laws, rather than merely announcing decrees as he had done in the past. It would not be easy, though. Democracy was new to Brazil and would take some getting used to. To complicate matters, no party enjoyed an overall majority. The situation was made even worse by the antipathy of the UDN towards Vargas. They loathed him so much that they attempted to persuade senior military officers that his inauguration should not be allowed to go ahead as he had failed to win an absolute majority of the vote in the election. There was nothing in the 1946 Constitution to support this demand. The military were themselves divided on Vargas's re-election. A split had formed in their ranks between nationalists and opponents who were sarcastically dubbed *entreguistas* (capitulators). The nationalists sought industrial development in order to help the Brazilian economy flourish independently of international forces. This meant government investment in iron, transport, petroleum and communications but, in the nationalists' opinion, these vital industries would not have to rely on the foreign investment and influence that they considered a danger to Brazilian sovereignty. The *entreguistas* championed minimal state intervention and investment, believing that the nation would be better served by controlled exposure to foreign capital. Government expenditure would be limited if they had their way. Brazil faced serious economic problems and Vargas had made a campaign promise to deal with them. In 1951, Finance Minister Horacio Lafer (1900–65) announced the 'Lafer Plan', a scheme to direct investment towards basic industries, with particular emphasis on transport and energy. His strategy depended on foreign investment, even though Vargas had advocated economic nationalism since 1945. It was a controversial issue that exploded in a welter of debate after the passing of a bill in December 1951 creating a joint venture involving public and private finances to develop Brazil's oil resources. The government would own the majority of shares in a new company – Petrobrás (*Petróleos Brasileiros*). The Communists and the nationalists reacted angrily to the involvement of foreign capital, while Brazilian business interests supported the action, focused on attracting foreign capital to grow their businesses and intent on building good relations with trading partners, especially the United States. Many in the military were also keen on maintaining close ties to the USA, having developed good relations with its military during the war. They also wanted to be seen to be firmly on the side of the West in the Cold War. Nonetheless, the Brazilian people were captivated by the idea of economic independence and the slogan '*o petroléo é nosso*' ('the petrol is ours') became popular. Finally, in October 1953, Congress yielded to public pressure and passed a bill nationalising the Brazilian oil industry.

Vargas had relied, to a large extent, on urban workers and the unions for his re-election. He was going to look to them once again for the 1954 election which brought the issue of an increase in the minimum wage to the fore. Wages in 1953 represented only 53 per cent of what they had been ten years earlier. But there was also an urgent need to reduce inflation. To deal with this, Vargas turned to one of his most loyal supporters,

Osvaldo Aranha, appointing him Finance Minister. To the position of Minister of Labour, he appointed João Goulart (1919–76) whose father had been a neighbour in Rio Grande do Sul. Goulart had close ties with the unions and had been vice president of the Brazilian Labour Party. His appointment was a blatant attempt by Vargas to appeal to workers. The army was concerned about Goulart, though, suspecting him to have Communist sympathies and worrying that he would use the workers to seize power.

Aranha espoused austerity as a way of getting Brazil out of economic trouble while Goulart argued for an increase in the minimum wage to improve the lives of the workers. There was uproar – the middle classes objected to the notion of an increase and the armed forces expressed their disquiet about it, horrified that Goulart's proposal could mean that some workers would be better paid than junior officers. Criticism of Vargas increased, Carlos Lacerda (1914–77) of the UDN accusing the government of incompetence and corruption and suggesting that Vargas was about to launch a coup d'état to re-establish a dictatorship.

The End of Vargas

In February 1954, Vargas sacked Goulart following his proposal of a 100 per cent increase in the minimum wage, the dismissal implying implicit support for Aranha's austerity plan. To everyone's surprise, however, on May Day, Vargas announced in a speech at Petrópolis that there would, after all, be a 100 per cent increase in the minimum wage. It was a shameless appeal for support to the workers of Brazil. 'Today you are with the government,' he told them, 'tomorrow you will be the government.' (*Politics in Brazil 1930–1964: An Experiment in Democracy*, Thomas E Skidmore, New York, Oxford University Press, 2007) It was a significant moment, because it alienated both the middle class and the military. Carlos Lacerda denounced Vargas in the media, but the president remained firmly in control. It would be from within his own circle, finally, that an opportunity to get rid of him would arise.

On 5 August 1954, Lacerda was wounded in the foot in an assassination attempt in which Brazilian Air Force Major Rubens Vaz (1922–54) was killed. An investigation traced the assassination plan back to Gregório Fortunato (1900–62), commander of the presidential guard and a loyal servant to Vargas for more than thirty years. The investigation also uncovered numerous financial irregularities and connections with organised crime in which a number of Vargas's aides and advisers were implicated. Pressure began to mount on the president, including demonstrators demanding his resignation on a daily basis outside the presidential palace. Vargas denied all knowledge of the assassination attempt but, by 23 August, following the publication of a letter signed by 27 Brazilian generals demanding his resignation, it was evident that he had lost the support of the military. The president's response was dramatic and ultimately tragic. He had already warned those close to him that he would rather die than suffer the ignominy of being removed from office as had happened in 1945. The day after the generals presented him with their petition, he shot himself through the heart in his rooms in the presidential palace. Beside him was found a note claiming that his action was the result of pressure from 'international economic and financial groups'. He ended this last communication with:

'I fought against the looting of Brazil. I fought against the looting of the people. I have fought bare-breasted. The hatred, infamy and calumny did not beat down my spirit. I gave you my life. Now I offer my death. Nothing remains. Serenely I take the first step on the road to eternity and I leave my life to enter history.'

(Quoted in *A Documentary History of Brazil*, E Bradford Burns, New York, Knopf, 1966)

Vargas's suicide shocked the nation and crowds of people took to the streets of the country's towns and cities, attacking the American embassy in Rio de Janeiro as well as the offices of opposition newspapers and foreign financial institutions. Vargas was now viewed as a martyr and his reputation as 'father of the poor' was widely promulgated. This time, however, there was no coup, the army preferring instead to stand aside and allow the country to find a constitutional settlement to this particular crisis. Sworn in as president, Vice President João Fernandes Campos Café Filho (1899–1970) formed a cabinet consisting of a majority of UDN members. It was announced that there would be an election to find a new president in October 1955.

7

Flirting with Democracy
1954 to 1964

The parties began to nominate their candidates for the upcoming election. The PSD were first out of the blocks with their nomination of Juscelino Kubitschek (1902–76), former governor of Minas Gerais. Kubitschek was the son of a travelling salesman who walked out on his family when Kubitschek was only two. Raised by his mother who was of Czech and Roma descent, he trained as a doctor and was elected to the Chamber of Deputies in 1934. During the dictatorship of Vargas, he had returned to practising medicine but by 1940 was mayor of Belo Horizonte and in 1950 became governor of Minas Gerais. His campaign slogan in 1955 was the ambitious 'fifty years of progress in five'. He was a clever politician who also gained the support of the PTB. The UDN nominated another former member of the lieutenants' movement, General Juarez Távora (1898–1975).

Kubitschek's campaign promoted the use of private and public capital to drive economic development while Távora was against state intervention in the economy. The campaign itself was not without devious tricks but eventually Kubitschek came out on top by a narrow margin, receiving 36 per cent of the votes while Távora took 30 per cent. Ademar de Barros of the *Partido Social Progressista* (Social Progressive Party) or PSP gained 26 per cent and Plínio Salgado won 8 per cent for the AIB. João Goulart was elected vice president. As soon as the result was known, however, there were efforts to prevent it being implemented. This looked an even greater possibility when incumbent President Café Filho suffered a heart attack and the president of the Chamber of Deputies, Carlos Luz (1894–1961) replaced him. Luz and others wished to prevent Kubitschek and Goulart, whom they suspected of having Communist tendencies, from taking office. This persuaded army Marshal Henrique Lott (1894–1984) to order his troops to seize control of government buildings, radio stations and newspapers on 11 November 1955, to prevent the conspirators from taking control. That day, Congress announced that it was replacing Luz who had been president for just two days with the President of the Senate, Nereu Ramos (1888–1958). After Café Filho made an attempt to regain the presidency a short while later, Congress declared the country to be in a 'state of siege', a situation that prevailed for the next thirty days. Finally, on 31 January 1956, Kubitschek and Goulart were inaugurated.

Kubitschek's presidency persuaded Brazilians to think that perhaps their experiment with democracy was working, after all. As the new president's slogan of 'fifty years in five' resounded around the nation, there was an air of optimism that was justified by a degree of unfamiliar economic and political stability. President Kubitschek succeeded in securing huge investment from both inside Brazil and from abroad. Revenue from industrial production increased by 80 per cent. GDP grew at 7 per cent annually between 1955 and 1961, GDP per capita growth running at around three times that of the rest of Latin America. One of Kubitschek's most notable successes was the creation of a car-manufacturing industry based in São Paulo, many multinational corporations such as Overland, Ford, Volkswagen and General Motors constructing plants there. He even managed to enjoy cordial relations with the military.

Kubitschek published a *Programa de Metas* (Programme of Goals) that consisted of 31 objectives in the areas of energy, transport, food production, basic industry and education. The most ambitious of his objectives, however, was the construction of a new Brazilian federal capital in the state of Goiás in the centre of the country, six hundred miles northwest of Rio de Janeiro. It would be named Brasilia and would host the three branches of the federal government and the headquarters of many major Brazilian companies. The planning and development of the city, begun in 1956, was undertaken by three Brazilians – planner Lúcio Costa (1902–98), architect Oscar Niemeyer (1907–2012) and landscape architect Roberto Burle Marx (1909–94). On the symbolic date of 22 April 1960 – the 460th anniversary of Pedro Álvares Cabral's arrival off the coast of Brazil – it formally became the capital, a futuristic marvel, built from scratch, the architecture of which has earned it recognition as a UNESCO World Heritage Site.

Kubitschek's economic policy eventually fell into the trap that has caught many modern Brazilian governments. High spending certainly brought growth, but it also resulted in rising inflation. The costs of the construction of Brasilia and salary increases for government workers contributed greatly and in 1959, inflation reached 39.5 per cent. In 1958, he introduced economies, but that, of course, slowed growth and provided ammunition to his opponents as well as criticism from business and trade unions. Foreign interests were deeply concerned about Kubitschek's economic problems. In June 1959, after the breakdown of negotiations with the International Monetary Fund, to whom he had appealed for help, he gave a speech appealing to Brazilian nationalist sentiment in which he said:

'Brazil has come of age. We are no longer poor relatives obliged to stay in the kitchen and forbidden to enter the living room. We ask only collaboration of other nations. By making greater sacrifices we can attain political and principally economic independence without the help of others.'

(Quoted in *Politics in Brazil, 1930–64; an Experiment in Democracy*, Thomas E Skidmore, New York, Oxford University Press, 2007)

Quadros and Goulart

The candidates for the 1960 presidential election were army Marshal Henrique Lott, Jânio Quadros (1917–92) and Adhemar de Barros. Lott had been Minister of War in the governments of both Café Filho and Kubitschek. He was the candidate of the PSD and received the backing of the PTB when it became known that João Goulart would be his vice-presidential running mate. While Lott was inexperienced at campaigning, the former governor of São Paulo, Jânio Quadros, nominated by the UDN, was an exuberant character who had enjoyed a meteoric rise to prominence during the 1950s, marketing himself as a political outsider, a champion of open and honest government. He galvanised the anti-Vargas elite and the middle class while also winning the hearts of the working class. The symbol of his campaign was a broom, signalling his desire to sweep dishonest and corrupt politicians from office. Barros was the candidate of the PSP but was thought unlikely to win many votes outside his home state of São Paulo. Ultimately, the huge effort that Quadros put into his campaign paid off. He won 48 per cent of the 11,700,000 votes cast. Lott received 28 per cent and Barros 24 per cent. It was a sensational victory and a wake-up call for Brazil's politicians. Goulart was again elected vice president and the two men were inaugurated in the new capital, Brasilia, the first to be so honoured.

Although he had been nominated by the UDN, Quadros had paid little attention to the party, preferring to distance himself from party politics. Therefore, although the UDN had nominally come to power, they had little influence over the new president. It did not matter, because Quadros enjoyed poor relations with all the political parties in Congress. The presidential palace was now located in Brasilia, the newly constructed Alvorada Palace, designed in the modernist style by Oscar Niemeyer, and Quadros seemed almost marooned there, governing in splendid isolation. He responded badly to criticism and was awkward with people which made doing business with him somewhat difficult. There were a great many doubts as to whether he actually had a coherent political programme. He declared inflation to be his principal target but his economic policy was muddled. He made cuts in federal spending but sought loans from the International Monetary Fund and the Alliance for Progress, an organisation initiated by US President John F Kennedy (1917–63) to foster economic cooperation between the United States and the countries of Latin America. In foreign affairs, he reduced Brazil's ties to the United States, choosing instead to develop relations with the nations of the Third World, especially those of Africa. Controversially, he also moved Brazil closer to Communist countries such as Cuba which he visited in 1960. Carlos Lacerda was particularly angered by the visit of Cuban revolutionary, Che Guevara (1928–67), to Brazil in 1961 when he was awarded the *Ordem Nacional do Cruzeiro do Sul* (Order of the Southern Cross), a Brazilian order of chivalry. Meanwhile, Vice President Goulart visited both the Soviet Union and China.

President Quadros had encountered nothing but hostility from Congress and was not a man blessed with a surfeit of patience. Lacerda was a particularly irritating thorn in his flesh. A few days after the presentation of the Southern Cross to Che Guevara, Lacerda appeared on television, heavily criticising Quadros and claiming that he was planning a coup d'état. The following afternoon, 25 August 1961, Quadros shocked the nation by unexpectedly announcing his resignation. He had been in office for a mere seven months. Like Vargas, he claimed in his letter of resignation that he had been subject to 'foreign forces' that had prevented him from carrying out his policies and achieving economic independence. 'I wanted Brazil for the Brazilians,' he wrote.

To this day, it is unclear why Quadros took this drastic action. The best guess seems to be that he hoped that by provoking a political crisis, he would force the military, who would never accept Goulart as president, to take control for a short time. They would then reinstate him, he believed, at the head of a more authoritarian regime. He was sadly mistaken and once again Brazil was plunged into crisis. Quadros went into exile in Europe, greatly distancing himself from any support he might have at home. Congress enthusiastically accepted his resignation and appointed Pascoal Ranieri Mazzilli (1910–75), president of the Chamber of Deputies, as acting president. Meanwhile, a dazed Brazilian populace showed little sympathy for Quadros, accusing him of having abandoned his responsibilities. The trade unions and leftist elements were also not sad to see him go as it meant that they could now throw their support behind Goulart. Meanwhile, there was division in military ranks about what to do next. Some, such as War Minister Odílio Denys (1892–1985), feared Goulart's Communist ties and were resolved that he should not be president, but others, such as General José Machado Lopes (1900–90), commander of the Brazilian Third Army based in Rio Grande do Sul, supported Goulart. Goulart, meanwhile, was on a trade mission to China and as he hurriedly made his way home, civil war seemed a possibility. But, as had happened before in Brazilian history, compromise won the day. The military yielded to the notion of Goulart becoming president and Congress agreed to amend the constitution to make Brazil a parliamentary democracy instead of a presidential one, greatly reducing presidential power. A Council of Ministers, responsible to the legislature, was created that was to be headed by a prime minister who would share executive power with the president. On 7 September 1961, João Belchior Marques Goulart was finally inaugurated as President of Brazil.

Naturally, Goulart was dismayed by the circumstances in which he assumed office and he resolved to do away with the parliamentary system and the restrictions on his powers as quickly as possible. There were many who agreed with him, believing him to have been treated unfairly. The Brazilian

Socialist Party and the National Student Union came out in support, denouncing the amendment as unconstitutional. Moreover, the entire drama was played out against the backdrop of a serious economic crisis that many thought would be better managed by a strong government. Eventually, the military agreed to permit a plebiscite of the Brazilian people and on 6 January 1963, a remarkable 9 million out of the 12 million who cast a vote demonstrated their support for a presidential system. Goulart's presidential powers were restored. For him, it was a personal triumph and one that he believed gave him a popular mandate. Before long, however, he had begun to alienate even his own supporters with a radical programme of economic and social welfare reforms – the *reformas de base* (basic reforms) as he called them. These included agrarian and urban reform and the extension of the right to vote to the illiterate and to enlisted men, a tactic he hoped would increase support for his populist government. There were also nationalist measures that provided for increased state intervention in financial matters. Industries such as meat-packing and pharmaceuticals were to be nationalised.

By this time, however, Brazil was in the midst of increasing social, economic and political crisis. The congressional elections of 1962 emphasised the increasing fragmentation of Brazilian politics. The PSD was still the largest party in Congress but failed to win an overall majority. There were strikes and demonstrations and a growth in rural movements such as peasant leagues. Francisco Julião (1915–99), a lawyer and politician from Pernambuco, led one such movement, trying to mobilise and organise the peasants. He created a centralised organisation and leagues began to appear throughout the country. In 1963, Goulart signed a law that gave official status to rural workers, regulated the working day, provided paid holidays and ensured that workers be paid the minimum wage. He calculated that this reform would make rural workers better off and would create greater demand for Brazilian manufactured goods.

Goulart announced the launch of a 'Three-Year Plan' in January 1963 that he declared would provide growth and tackle inflation. It was effectively the same policy as Kubitschek had pursued, of using growth to beat down inflation. It made little difference, however, and inflation continued to rise. Meanwhile, attempts to obtain loans from the United States were hindered by Brazil's reputation for economic nationalism and its previous fiscal performance. Then, when Goulart irresponsibly increased the wages of civil servants and military officers by 70 per cent against the recommendation in the Three-Year Plan of just 40 per cent, inflation leapt. In 1963, it was running at 80 per cent annually and investment from overseas was dramatically declining.

Goulart's plan to expropriate large tracts of agricultural land and redistribute it to the peasants had a number of objectives. Of course, it would please those of the electorate who benefited and would make them amenable to Goulart's ongoing political aims. It would also help to bring an end, he hoped, to the political disruption that was taking place in the countryside, a response to Francisco Juliao and his peasant leagues. Landowners were, naturally, against it and the president and Congress were set against each other over the issue when the Agrarian Reform Bill was put before Congress in March 1963. Goulart, faced with Congress's intransigence, decided not to follow the example of Quadros and resign. Instead, he appealed directly to the Brazilian people in a series of huge rallies watched by millions on television. At the first of these, on 13 March 1964, in front of a crowd of 150,000, and flanked by left-wingers and Communists, Goulart announced the seizure of 'under-utilised' land. The underlying current suggested that if the politicians did not agree to this then the people of Brazil would depose them. There was alarm at this turn of events from the landed elite and the established political parties, deeply resentful of the growing influence of left-wing groups and the unions. Foreign investors – especially the United States – began to take fright at the apparent growth of Communist influence in Brazil. On 19 March, opponents of Goulart's government took to the streets, 500,000 people joining the 'March of the Family with God for Liberty' in São Paulo, protesting against what they saw as the president's betrayal of Christian family values and his Communist links.

The military looked on with its usual interest. Goulart had, like many of his predecessors, appointed his own men to senior positions and had also cultivated a following amongst the *sargentos* (non-commissioned officers) and enlisted men, leaving the officers isolated and angry, convinced that Goulart might be about to stage a coup to establish himself as dictator. The army Chief-of-Staff, General Humberto de Alencar Castelo Branco (1897–1967), later president of Brazil, let it be known that the army would not help him achieve this, to 'submit the nation to Moscow Communism', as he described it to senior officers. Matters began to come to a head when, following a mutiny by a number of sailors in Rio de Janeiro, Goulart sacked his Navy Minister and granted an amnesty to those who had mutinied. The army could take no more. On 31 March, General Carlos Luís Guedes mobilised his infantry units and set out from Minas Gerais to mount an attack on Rio and restore constitutional government to Brazil. There was wholehearted support for his action from other military commanders and from politicians. On 1 April, government buildings in Rio de Janeiro and Brasilia were seized, persuading President Goulart to flee three days later to Rio Grande do Sul and on to exile in Uruguay where he died of a heart attack in 1974. Congress declared the presidency vacant, putting the president of the Chamber of Deputies, Ranieri Mazzilli, in temporary charge once more.

Brazil had enjoyed democracy for just nineteen years. Once again the military men were in charge and this time they meant business.

8

Military Government, Democracy and Economic Miracles 1964 to Present Day

Military Rule

Of course, as we have seen, this was not the first time that the military had intervened in Brazilian history. There had already been military interventions in 1930, 1945, 1954, 1955 and 1961. This time, however, although they had intervened to maintain social order and prevent Communism from becoming more influential, they were also conscious that there was a danger of civil war. It was thought that Goulart's supporters were ready to resort to violence in the event of a right-wing coup. For this reason, the soldiers did not withdraw to their barracks after the coup, as had usually been the case. Instead, the military formed a junta made up of three generals, one each from the army, the navy and the air force. Their interim government was to be known as *Comando Supremo Revolucionário* (Revolutionary Supreme Command). At its head was General Arturo da Costa e Silva (1899–1969) who had been removed from command of the 4th Army by Goulart after putting down left-wing student demonstrations in Brazil's Northeast. The military takeover was welcomed by many elements of Brazilian society including the media, the Catholic Church, businessmen, politicians and a group of wealthy women who feared high prices for consumer goods and improved rights for their servants. As time went on, however, and the extent of the repression that was being imposed on the country became clear, many changed their minds. The United States was extremely supportive of the coup, however, and would continue to support the dictators who ruled Brazil until 1988 when democracy was restored.

The coup of 1964 brought the first of what were called 'national security regimes' in which generals tried to change the nature of the state and society. Other South American countries would later copy the Brazilian example, Uruguay from 1973 to 1985, Chile from 1973 to 1990 and Argentina from 1976 to 1983. They all sought economic growth through stability and control, even though this meant that the individual human rights of anyone who opposed them were ignored. Repression was the order of the day. The generals took advantage of the disarray in which the opposition found itself and launched *Operacão Limpeza* (Operation Clean-up), arresting and imprisoning union activists, student leaders and left-wing politicians. On 11 April 1964, Humberto de Alencar Castelo Branco, an army marshal who had spent 300 days in combat zones as a member of the Brazilian Expeditionary Force during World War Two, was elected first president of the military regime. Castelo Branco was new to politics but enjoyed close ties with the American embassy. He used the motto 'development and national security' for his government. Military officers remained in control of the executive, but civilian technocrats were also co-opted into government, men such as noted economist Roberto de Oliveira Campos (1917–2001) who accepted the post of Minister of Planning and Economic Coordination. Campos sought to stabilise the Brazilian economy with the objective of reducing inflation by 10 per cent within two years and achieving zero inflation thereafter. He was relatively successful, bringing it down from 100 per cent in 1964 to 28 per cent in 1967.

The junta ruled through a set of exceptional measures – Institutional Acts – that initially did little to change the way the country was governed. But they had begun a rewrite of the constitution and in 1967 it was ratified by a Congress from which any element of opposition had been erased. This constitution stipulated that the president would be elected by an electoral college, but only military leaders could be candidates. The president was given the right to govern by decree, regardless of whether the legislature was in session. There were sections of the constitution that guaranteed individual rights, but these were either conveniently ignored over the next few years or were amended by special decree as the regime became increasingly repressive. That year Brazil also changed its name – from the Republic of the United States of Brazil to the Federative Republic of Brazil (*República Federativa do Brasil*).

The world experienced a great deal of turmoil in 1968. The North Vietnamese launched the Tet Offensive against US forces fighting the Vietnam War, demonstrating that they were capable of victory. Student protest erupted across the world, calling for an end to American involvement in Vietnam, amongst other things. In Brazil, tens of thousands of students took to the streets in protest at the rule of the generals. They were joined by working class people in São Paulo and Rio de Janeiro, leading the military rulers to invent a 'Communist threat' and come down hard on the demonstrators.

Institutional Act Number Two had already dissolved all existing political parties, replacing them with two new ones – the 'opposition' party, the *Movimento Democrático Brasileiro* (Brazilian Democratic Movement) or MDB and the government party, the *Aliança Renovadora Nacional* (National Renewal Alliance Party), commonly known as ARENA. The first Institutional Act had introduced what was known as *cassacão* (cassation) by which 'political undesirables' could be barred from holding political office and from voting in elections. Amongst its 400 or so victims were former presidents Goulart, Kubitschek and Quadros and prominent leftist politicians such as Luís Carlos Prestes. A new agency, the *Serviço Nacional de Informações* (National Intelligence Service) or SNI, was created to deal with domestic security. This much-feared body, reporting directly to the president, carried out investigations and ordered the arrest of many deemed to be subversive, using violence and terror to fulfill its aims.

Dark Days

On 15 March 1967, General Artur da Costa e Silva replaced Castelo Branco as president. Costa e Silva had indicated that he wanted to 'humanise' the revolution, raising hopes that there might be an easing of the repression that had characterised Castelo Branco's term of office. When his cabinet was announced, however, the important jobs had been allocated to hardliners. There would be no relaxation it seemed, a realisation that was met by criticism from such as Dom Helder Câmara (1909–99), Archbishop of Recife and Olinda who also remonstrated with the government regarding its neglect of the poor. A year later, the discontent would erupt in demonstrations, a strike by metalworkers in Belo Horizonte and a series of student rallies. Costa e Silva responded to the anti-government feeling with violence and arrests. The situation deteriorated further when a constitutional stalemate was arrived at with Congress over its refusal to lift the parliamentary immunity of MDB deputy and government critic Marcio Moreira Alves (1936–2009) in December 1968. He had recommended in a speech that, as an act of protest at the military regime, young women should refuse to dance with military cadets. In response, Costa e Silva issued Institutional Act No. 5 (AI–5) on 13 December 1968. It suspended the constitution, removed the right of *habeas corpus* for crimes against 'national security', closed all branches of government – including Congress – introduced censorship of the media and declared Brazil to be in a state of emergency. The cassation of more politicians was announced, all elections were suspended and state militia and police forces were put under federal government control. Public criticism of the government or the armed forces was made illegal in a decree published in March 1969 and from then until

1975 was a dark period for Brazil. Artists, intellectuals, writers and world-famous musicians such as Caetano Veloso (b. 1942) and Gilberto Gil (b. 1942) chose to work against the junta from exile rather than remain in their homeland where they risked torture, execution or disappearance.

Another crisis erupted on 29 August 1969, when President Costa e Silva suffered a stroke. The 1967 Constitution stipulated that in the event of a president being incapacitated, he should be replaced by the vice president. The vice president in this case, however, was Pedro Aleixo (1901–75), a civilian who had not been entirely supportive of Institutional Act No. 5. The generals conveniently ignored the constitution, nominating instead General Emilio Garrastazú Médici (1905–85), commander of the Third Army in Rio Grande do Sul. Congress was quickly reconvened to rubber-stamp the generals' decision and Médici was sworn in to serve the remainder of Costa e Silva's term of office as well as a further five-year term. Yet another new constitution was introduced that confirmed all the legislation decreed since 1967. Médici believed firmly that military rule was justified by the need to maintain order and implement the policies followed since the coup of 1964. The generals, nonetheless, hankered for legitimacy and the support of the people. To this end, they announced elections to the National Congress and state assemblies to be held in 1970 but, of course, the candidates were all members of the two permitted political parties – ARENA and the MDB. There was a sizeable protest vote in the elections with around 30 per cent of all ballot papers being either blank or spoiled, but ARENA won a majority in Congress.

New levels of intimidation and terror were reached during the Médici administration with the army and police carrying out 'search-and-arrest' operations whose victims were usually tortured and imprisoned without trial. Notorious 'death squads' viciously eliminated suspected 'subversives' in Rio de Janeiro and São Paulo. Many innocent civilians were included in the deadly statistics in what General Carlos Brilhante Ustra (b.1932) described as a 'war without uniforms, situated in the streets, where the enemy was mixed with the general population, [where] the police cannot distinguish by sight the terrorists from good citizens'. Salvadorian architect Carlos Marighella (1911–69) led a small urban guerrilla movement, *Ação Libertadora Nacional* (Action for National Liberation) or ALN that carried out acts of sabotage, including the kidnapping of the US ambassador, Charles Burke Elbrick (1908–83), in an action shared with the *Movimento Revolucionário 8 de Outubro* (Revolutionary Movement 8th October) or MR–8. Elbrick was released after seventy-eight hours in exchange for the freedom of fifteen imprisoned leftists while Marighella was eventually shot dead by police officers in São Paulo in 1969. To combat the increasing terrorist threat, the government employed around 200,000 people in the SNI and other anti-terrorist agencies. Ultimately, the terrorists were never a serious threat, failing to mount a united front and lacking effective leadership. The only consequence of their actions was that it provided the government with justification for its hardline approach.

Nonetheless, Médici benefited from the wave of good feeling that swept across the country when the great Brazilian footballer, Pele, led his country to a stunning World Cup triumph in Mexico in 1970, football being an abiding passion of the Brazilian people. Naturally, the Médici government claimed credit for this and worked hard at maximising PR benefit from anything it could, using the *Assessorial Especial de Relações Publicas* (Special Advisory Body on Public Relations) that had been created in 1968. Médici also claimed credit for the growth in the economy that had been fostered by the *paulista* economist Delfim Neto (b.1928) while he was Minister of Finance in the Costa e Silva administration. Neto had done it by reducing interest rates, and facilitating the investment of large amounts of foreign capital into basic industries at very favourable rates to the investors as well as into the development of the infrastructure (including the construction of the Transamazonian Highway). This helped to stimulate growth during the six years in which Médici was in office. It became known as the 'Brazilian Miracle' and led to Médici boasting that Brazil would soon become a 'world power'. Sadly, it was no more than a 'quick fix' and saddled Brazil with an unmanageably large amount of debt and inflation. There were, of course, successes. Steel production more than trebled between 1964 and 1976 and car production went up by more than 500 per cent. The traditional reliance on exports of coffee was dissipated by the export of a variety of goods. However, the gap between rich and poor grew inexorably and poverty was rife. Rapid industrialisation had brought people to the cities where sanitation, electricity, water and other resources became severely stretched. Whereas in 1950, 64 per cent of the Brazilian population had lived in the countryside, by 1980 only 33 per cent were rural. In effect, instead of easing the plight of the poor, the military government had handed the Brazilian economy over to foreign investors in order to obtain military hardware that helped it to create a powerful army, air force and navy. Naturally, this made its South American neighbours uneasy but the lack of any real expansionist ambitions suggests that this formidable force was simply to be used against the Brazilian people, to maintain power for the generals.

Around this time, a new approach to religion, known as liberation theology began to emerge in the Catholic Church in Latin America, with many nuns and priests championing the rights of the poor and disadvantaged. It was especially popular in Brazil where the poor were suffering greatly under military rule. In the 1970s, the clergy – leaders, after all, of the largest Catholic population in the world – became ardent critics of the generals and made sure that international media and organisations were aware of the abuses taking place in the country.

Decompression

In 1973, with Médici's lengthy term of office coming to an end, the military high command chose a man widely thought of as a moderate, General Ernesto Geisel (1907–96), to succeed him. A native of Rio Grande do Sul, like his predecessor, Geisel had participated in the 1930 revolution and the Vargas regime and had played a vital role in the 1964 coup d'état. At the time of his selection for the nation's top job, he was president of Petrobrás, the state-owned oil company. He was endorsed as a candidate by ARENA while the MDB backed an alternative anti-government candidate, Ulysses Guimãraes (1916–92). Needless to say, on 15 January 1974, Geisel romped home by 400 votes to 76 in the National Congress. But by this time, elements of the military were beginning to question the authoritarian nature of military rule. There was no longer the threat of terrorism that had been present at the end of the 1960s and the use of torture by the regime was coming under greater scrutiny and facing mounting criticism both at home and abroad. The influential General Golbery do Couto e Silva (1911–87), a key adviser to Geisel, argued that the armed forces were being damaged by government and counselled the president to encourage civilian participation in politics. Geisel paid heed to what he was saying, launching a new strategy of gradual change that came to be known as *decompressão* (decompression).

Elections to the National Congress were announced for November 1974 with candidates permitted to present their views in the media. The results, however, did not go quite the way the government had anticipated. In fact, the 'anti-government' MDB succeeded in greatly reducing ARENA's majority in the National Congress and on this occasion many fewer people chose to spoil their ballot papers than in recent elections. This surprise strengthened the position of hardliners in the military, and led Geisel to restrict access to the media for candidates in the 1976 municipal elections, denying the opposition the opportunity to air their views and policies. This decree was later applied to federal and state elections. In April 1977, as state governorship elections approached, Geisel used the powers provided by IA–5 to introduce what became known as the 'April Package' that maintained the practice of indirect elections. This measure also provided for directly appointed senators and helped to maintain a government majority in the Senate.

In 1973, the world's economy had been thrown into chaos when the members of the Organisation of Petroleum Exporting Countries (OPEC) declared an oil embargo in response to the United States supplying arms to Israel during the Yom Kippur War with Egypt and Syria that year. This created a sharp rise in oil prices that was damaging to many economies including that of Brazil. By 1974, the oil crisis was hitting Brazil hard, hampering growth and stalling the 'economic miracle'. Geisel tried to counter it by committing to promoting growth and re-distributing income in a way that would benefit the poor. Later in that decade, there were major changes in line with 'decompression' when IA–5 was revoked, *habeas corpus* was re-introduced for those arrested on political grounds and censorship was eased. As many Brazilian political exiles returned from overseas, the military hardliners were far from happy. In October 1977, when the principal opponent of 'decompression', General Sylvio Frota (1910–96), was found to be planning to succeed Geisel, the president demonstrated his authority and impatience with opponents by sacking him from his cabinet. Instead, his choice, General João Figueiredo (1918–99), head of the NIS, was nominated in April 1978 by ARENA while the MDB selected General Euler Bentes Monteiro (1917–2002) as its candidate. Figueiredo was duly elected president by the legislature in October 1978 and inaugurated on 15 March 1979 to serve a six-year term.

Abertura – Political 'Opening'

In protest at rising inflation and demanding higher wages, car workers in São Paulo had staged a strike in 1978, ten years after the last withdrawal of labour of any importance. Soon, the cessation of work had spread to other professions and, in 1979, more than three million workers, egged on by the Roman Catholic Church, now at the forefront of protest against the generals, downed tools. Fortunately, however, Figueiredo had expressed support for 'decompression' during the election campaign, stating his intention 'to make of this country a democracy'. He also hinted at the possibility of direct popular elections to Congress. 'Decompression' was now known as *'abertura'*, meaning the 'opening' of the political system. In line with this, Figueiredo offered an amnesty to everyone who had been accused of political crimes since 1961, an offer quickly approved by Congress in order to ease the path to more democratic government. Censorship was ended, Brazilians enjoying freedom of speech for the first time in many years. The president also approved the freedom to establish political parties, abolishing the two-party system that Castelo Branco had introduced in 1965. Those in power clung to the hope that the opposition would be too disorganised, allowing ARENA to maintain its majority in Congress.

The two existing parties re-modelled themselves, ARENA becoming the *Partido Democrático Social* (Social Democratic Party) or PDS while the MDB transformed itself into the *Partido do Movimento Democrático Brasileiro* (Brazilian Democratic Movement Party) or PMDB. The *Partido Popular* (Popular Party) or PP was formed by some members of the MDB and ARENA. On the Left, there were three parties – the PTB, now led by Getúlio Vargas's niece, Ivete Vargas (1927–84); the *Partido Democratico Trabalhista* (Democratic Labour Party) or PDT led by Leonel Brizola (1922–2004); and the *Partido dos Trabalhadores* (Workers' Party) or PT, created by the trade unions with Luiz

Inácio 'Lula' da Silva (b.1945) the president of the São Bernardo Metalworkers Union as its charismatic head. Within a decade it would become a major political force in the country.

President Figueiredo was under intense pressure from hardliners in the military not to allow direct elections but, in 1981, he announced them for Congress, state governors, assemblies, mayors and municipalities, to be held in November 1982. This decision was made easier because of a bombing outrage that showed military hardliners in a very poor light. In May 1981, two soldiers died when a bomb exploded accidentally in the car in which they were travelling. They had been en route to a music concert where the bomb was going to be detonated with the intention of killing and injuring civilians. It was immediately suspected by an outraged public that the army had probably been behind a number of recent explosions.

In the elections that took place in 1982, as expected, the conservative PDS – formerly ARENA – won in rural areas and the more liberal PMDB – the old MDB - triumphed in urban areas, winning the cities. But ten of the twenty-two elections for governor were won by the opposition parties, including Leonel Brizola winning Rio de Janeiro state for the PDT. The PDS maintained its majority in the Senate but lost control of the Chamber of Deputies.

Return to Civilian Rule

In 1981, President Figueiredo suffered a stroke, leading to a lack of leadership at the head of the country for several years. When he consistently refused to name a successor, a movement began demanding direct elections for the office of president in 1985. Massive public rallies were staged at which the slogan *'diretas já'* ('direct elections now') rang out. The amendment to introduce such elections was defeated in the Chamber of Deputies nine days later but the military, demoralised and hampered by Figueiredo's weakness, failed to nominate a military candidate for the election. Instead it would be contested by two civilians – Paulo Maluf (b.1931), a wealthy businessman and former governor of São Paulo for the PDS and Minas Gerais Governor Tancredo Neves (1910–85), backed by the PMDB.

Maluf was a controversial choice that led to a number of PDS members, including Vice President Aureliano Chaves (1929–2003) and José Sarney (b.1930), PDS leader in the Senate, breaking away and establishing a new political party – the *Partido da Frente Liberal* (Liberal Front Party) or PFL which joined with the PMDB to create the *Aliança Democrática* (Democratic Alliance), in support of Tancredo Neves. Sarney, a supporter of the military government, was nominated by them for vice president. Tancredo had already agreed with the military that revenge would not be sought for the years of authoritarian rule and brutality if he were to secure the presidency. His campaign spoke of a 'New Republic' and promised a fight against fraud and corruption. The military and President Figueiredo gave him their backing.

On 15 January 1985, the Electoral College of 686 members cast their votes to select the man who would lead them back to civilian rule. Tancredo Neves won by 480 votes (72.4 per cent) to 180 (27.3 per cent), with 26 delegates, mostly from the PT, the Workers' Party, abstaining. The election had been coloured by Maluf's reputation as a ruthless politician who had used his wealth to achieve success. Although he could be viewed as something of a man of the past – he had, after all, served as Minister of Justice in the Vargas administration and as prime minister for João Goulart – Tancredo was at least perceived to be a man of integrity. There was great enthusiasm, therefore, for Tancredo's vision of a 'New Republic'. The nation was shocked, however, when he became seriously ill on the eve of his inauguration. After several operations, he died on 21 April.

As stipulated by the constitution, the presidency passed to the next in line, Vice President José Sarney who was inaugurated as Brazil's first civilian head of state in twenty-one years. From Maranhão, Sarney had been one of a group of young UDN politicians who emerged in the 1950s, determined to fight corruption and dishonesty in government. During military rule, he had become president of the pro-government party, ARENA, and after the fall of the generals had participated in the creation of the Liberal Front Party that had replaced ARENA. His affiliation with ARENA and loyalty to the military government over the years undoubtedly made it easier for the armed forces to accept civilian rule but those very same things led to a spiky relationship with Congress. He was also considered lucky to have achieved the top position and was generally thought to lack the credibility and authority of the late Tancredo Neves.

The most pressing matter when Sarney took office was, without doubt, economic recovery and he spoke earnestly of his desire to cut inflation – rising between 1980 and 1985 from an annual rate of 86.3 per cent to 248 per cent – and stimulate the public sector's desire to invest. In February 1986, he launched a package of measures that became known as 'the *Cruzado* Plan' that was designed to rapidly bring inflation under control. A readjustment and freeze were applied to prices, wages, rents and mortgage payments. Furthermore, a new unit of currency, the *cruzado* was introduced, rated at one *cruzado* to 1,000 *cruzeiros*. There was an immediate improvement with the rate of inflation falling to almost zero and signs of a consumer boom. A surge in economic growth followed and foreign exchange was brought under control. In the congressional and state elections of 1986, the Democratic Alliance was rewarded, winning all the state governorships and more than 75 per cent of all the seats in the Chamber of Deputies and the Senate. By the end of 1986, however, inflation was on the rise again and it was suggested that voters had been fooled. Further economic plans – the Bresser Plan of 1987 and the Summer Plan of 1989 – failed to prevent stagnation and by the last year of Sarney's increasingly unpopular presidency, inflation had soared to more than 1,000 per cent. Brazil appeared to be out of control, especially when strikers were involved in violent clashes with the police. Meanwhile, a new constitution was approved and promulgated on 5 October 1988, but it changed little in the way the country was governed apart from promoting decentralisation, returning power and funds to the states and the municipalities. A run-off electoral system was introduced and the franchise was expanded to include sixteen-year-olds.

In 1989, direct popular elections for the presidency took place for the first time since 1960. With the lifting of restrictions on the formation of political parties, there was a plethora of new parties and candidates, twenty-two candidates in all. The resulting confusion regarding ideologies and policies led the Brazilian people to focus more on the individual personalities involved than the political party they represented. Leonel Brizola was standing again for the PDT and Lula da Silva once again represented the PT. Senator Mário Covas (1930–2001) stood on behalf of the *Partido da Social Democracia Brasileira* or PSDB (Brazilian Social Democracy Party) and *paulista* sociologist and politician, Fernando Henrique Cardoso (b.1930) represented a new group made up of former members of the PMDB. Standing out from the other candidates, however, was the political outsider, the tall, handsome forty-year-old Fernando Collor de Mello (b.1949), governor of the small Northeastern state of Alagoas, representing the tiny *Partido de Reconstrução Nacional* (Party of National Reconstruction) or PRN. As governor, Collor had gained popularity and national prominence through cutting public expenditure. His campaign advocated a moral crusade to eradicate corruption in government and in charismatic television appearances he promised to sweep away the officials and civil servants known as *marajás* (maharajas) whom he claimed were not only overpaid; they were also defrauding the state. His message held great appeal for an electorate of which the majority was below the age of thirty, with only 15 per cent being older than 50. In the first round of voting, Collor won most votes with Lula narrowly easing out

Brizola for second place and the opportunity to participate in the run-off. Collor maintained his lead in the second round of voting, taking 35.1 million votes – 53 per cent – against Lula's 31.1 million. The former senator from Minas Gerais, Itamar Franco (1930–2011) was elected vice president. Brazil's first democratically elected president in twenty-nine years was inaugurated in March 1990.

Controlling inflation was, as ever, the main task for the new president who, on his first day in office, launched a collection of economic reforms and anti-inflation plans known officially as the New Brazil Plan, but popularly described as the *Plano Collor*. It brought an immediate reduction in inflation which had been running at 30,000 per cent when he took office, fell to 400 per cent in 1991 but rose once more in 1992 to more than 1,000 per cent.

In May 1992, just a year into Collor's term of office, his integrity was called into question when it emerged that his campaign treasurer Paulo César Farias (1945–96) was involved in fraud. Collor's own brother, Pedro, accused the president of condoning a scheme where individuals were given preferential treatment in exchange for payment. There was further outrage when it emerged that the president's family were also implicated. A Commission of Enquiry was set up and in response President Collor appeared on television asking for the support of the Brazilian people against what he described as a 'coup'. People were disgusted, however, especially in view of the high-minded electoral campaign Collor had run. The report of the commission found that the president had, indeed, benefited financially from Farias's scheme, leading to a movement for his impeachment and removal from office. On 29 September 1992, he was impeached by the Chamber of Deputies by 441 votes to 38. He resigned the presidency on 29 December just before the start of the impeachment proceedings. Found guilty of abuse of political power, he was banned from political activity for eight years and replaced by Vice President Itamar Franco. The transition was peaceful, the armed forces watching from the sidelines without interfering.

Inflation was running at 2,670 per cent in the year after President Franco stepped into Collor's shoes. He made Fernando Henrique Cardoso his Minister of Finance and, after consultation with economists, the new minister launched the *Plano Real* (*Real* Plan) in an effort to achieve a balanced budget. As part of this, a new unit of currency, the *real*, was introduced, in place of the new *cruzeiro*. Cardoso's approach was a gradual one and he did not impose a wage- or price-freeze, arguing that these represented no more than short-term fixes. The value of the *real* was tied to that of the US dollar in an effort to prevent the all-too-frequent devaluation of the Brazilian currency. By making foreign imports cheaper, he would also keep inflation at manageable levels. During 1994, inflation was halved; by 1996, it was down to 22 per cent; in 1997 it was just 4 per cent and the following year for a few months it reached zero. Budget deficits were reduced and exports increased, particularly with the countries – Argentina, Uruguay and Paraguay – of the new free-trade zone, Mercosul (*Mercado Comum do Sul*), of which Brazil was a founding member.

Cardoso had been a frequent critic of the military regime in Brazil, a highly respected academic and intellectual who was able to use contacts with important people involved in human rights issues around the world. As such, he could be said to have played an important role in bringing about the downfall of the military government. He had gone into exile after the military coup, but returned to be a professor at the left-wing University of São Paulo. All of this helped to make him favourite to win the presidential election of 1994. He was believed to be the only man with enough support to stop the left-wing Lula finally becoming president. President Franco gave him his backing as did a coalition of political parties, including the PDSB, the PFL and the PTB. In the campaign, Cardoso showed that he had renounced his past on the left of Brazilian politics, but expressed support for a programme of social reforms and environmental initiatives and promised cuts to spending on the armed forces if elected. In the first round of voting on 3 October, he won the election outright with an overall majority of 54.4 per cent, 34 million votes against Lula da Silva's 17 million, enabling him to claim a popular mandate for his policies. To this day, he is the only president since direct popular elections were reintroduced in 1989 to win the presidency without having to resort to a run-off.

Cardoso – or 'FHC' as he was popularly known – took office in January 1995 and ruled with the backing of an unusually broad coalition of the parties which had supported him in the election, plus the centrist PMDB and the right-wing PP which joined him after the election. This often made for difficulties in Congress even though his coalition held an overwhelming majority of seats, but he benefited from the fact that by the time he entered office inflation had been reduced to only 1 per cent per annum. He worked to reduce the role of the state in the Brazilian economy, controversially expanding the privatisation programme that had been begun by President Collor, and seeming to go back on the position he had adopted as an academic. He successfully guided the country through a series of financial crises and also ordered the declassification of military files concerning Operation Condor, a campaign of political repression and terror perpetrated for several decades by some of the right-wing dictatorships of South America. By the end of the 1990s, Brazil was the tenth-largest national economy in the world. Doubts remained, however, fuelled by fears about the effect of the globalisation of the world economy on Brazil, as well as other ongoing concerns.

Brazil at the End of the Twentieth Century

The population of Brazil increased from 71 million in 1960 to 119 million in 1980; by the turn of the century, it had reached 170 million. As health provision improved, life expectancy rose from 52 years in 1960 to 62 years in 1980. It should be pointed out, however, that when comparisons were made with other South American countries this statistic lost some of its shine. Argentina, for instance, enjoyed a life expectancy of 72 years. The Brazilian population, therefore, was becoming increasingly older, the proportion of people aged under 15 falling from 42 per cent to 35 per cent between 1970 and 1991. In 2000, Brazil was the world's fifth most populous nation and it has been projected that by 2050 its population will have grown to 250 million.

The region of the Centre-South was the country's most populous area, slightly more than half the entire population living there. The population of the Northeast continued to decline while the Centre-West and the North showed the greatest increases, the latter encouraged by the discovery of gold in Rondônia and improvements in infrastructure. In the 1960s, for the first time the proportion of Brazilians living in towns and cities passed 50 per cent. By the year 2000, that figure had reached almost 80 per cent, job prospects and the rapid growth of mechanisation in agriculture forcing people to leave the countryside and seek employment opportunities in Brazil's towns and cities.

In the mid 1950s, São Paulo replaced Rio de Janeiro as the country's most populous city. With more than 11 million inhabitants, it is now the seventh most populous city in the world. In fact, the metropolitan area of São Paulo is home to some 15 million people. 10 per cent of Brazilians live there. Rio, meanwhile, has a population of just over 6 million.

Between 1964 and 2000, Brazilians – especially the middle and upper classes – saw a rise in their standard of living brought about by the economic growth the country experienced during that time. They also enjoyed significant improvements in such things as sanitation. In 1950, only 16 per cent of homes had access to piped running water; by 1990, that figure had increased to 70 per cent. Similarly, the percentage of homes with electricity increased significantly in the second half of the twentieth century, from 25 per cent in 1950 to nearly 90 per cent by 1990. The number of Brazilian families with a car rose from 9 per cent in 1970 to almost 40 per cent in 1994.

Unfortunately, the gap between rich and poor also increased. The Workers' Party (PT) claimed in 1994 that as many as 60 million Brazilians were living in poverty, 32 million of that number in conditions in which they were unable to feed themselves and their families properly. Meanwhile, the wealthiest 5 per cent of the Brazilian population earned 35.8 per cent of total income in 1990, an increase of just over 8 per cent since 1960. The poor were hard hit by inflation and negligence by successive military governments. Breaking out of poverty was rendered practically impossible by their lack of education and, even if they did manage to find a job, it was highly probable that because trade union activity had been suppressed for so long, wages would be low and conditions poor. Protest was often met with violence from the authorities. Even after the return to civilian rule, matters did not greatly improve.

The worst poverty was in the countryside, but it was most visible in Brazil's cities where the neglect of proper town planning led to the haphazard siting of factories and, most apparent of all, the proliferation of *favelas* – shanty-towns. These soon became associated with violence and organised crime, as depicted in the internationally successful 2002 film *City of God*. They also became notorious for the gangs of homeless children who were victimised and brutalised by the police because of suspicions that they were engaged in criminal activities. With the uncontrolled spread of industrial development, smog and pollution also became major concerns as Brazil's cities grew in size and population.

There was a dramatic switch from agriculture to industry in the second half of the twentieth century. In 1950, 60 per cent of Brazilians worked in agriculture; by 1978, this had fallen to 36 per cent. Meanwhile, the development of Brazil's industries brought half a million new jobs a year, mainly in car manufacture, pharmaceuticals and construction, while the service sector brought a further million jobs a year. Agricultural workers were increasingly employed seasonally or temporarily, many *favela* inhabitants labouring on farms. The number of women in employment increased significantly, from 2.5 million in 1950 to more than 18 million by 1980. This vital additional income helped raise many families out of poverty and also contributed to a decline in the birthrate, also a result of the greater availability of birth control and abortion.

Since the 1980s, there had been an acknowledgement – even amongst the military – that poor educational provision was hampering the prospects for Brazil's economic future. In 1970, 15.9 million Brazilian children were in education, a number that had risen to 42 million by 1994. The standard of education at primary and secondary levels, however, remained poor and the dropout rate was high.

The issue of land became a thorny one in the second half of the twentieth century. Governments encouraged an increase in the production of sugar cane to be made into alcohol and other new crops that would bring foreign exchange. Massive estates were created by wealthy landowners and corporations, leaving migrant farmers with no access to good farming land. This gave rise to tensions that received international attention, for instance, when the political activist Francisco 'Chico' Mendes (1944–88) was murdered. Mendes had made enemies with his courageous efforts to protect the Amazon from exploitation by loggers and agricultural companies and his murder brought condemnation from around the world. He was not the only one to lose his life as a result of the land issue. Around 1,500 people died between 1964 and 1986 in trouble over land-grabbing which was often carried out with the support of local landowners and corrupt government officials. In the Centre-South, in the 1980s, peasants formed the *Movimento dos Trabalhadores Rurais Sem Terra* (Landless Rural Workers

Movement) or MST. Supported by the Catholic Church and the Workers' Party, their stated aim was '… agrarian reform in order to work, produce, and guarantee abundant food on the table of every Brazilian'. To achieve their aims, they occupied and cultivated some of the vast tracts of land that were not being farmed.

Tensions also emerged on the issue of race. White Brazilians liked to believe that Brazilian society was racially equal, but studies showed that 50 per cent of black Brazilians remained illiterate. Furthermore, a mere 2 per cent of that segment of society proceeded to higher education after secondary school. Blacks and people of mixed race – a significant 40 per cent of the entire population – were poorly represented in the higher echelons of government and the military. In the 1988 Constitution, measures had been taken to fight discrimination on the grounds of colour, but in 1990, only 12 non-whites were elected to the National Congress.

The government's attitude to the indigenous peoples in the second half of the twentieth century was even worse. As areas of the North were opened to commercial exploitation by farmers, miners and prospectors, their plight was ignored. Corruption and poor management by the Indian Protection Service, created to protect indigenous people, but more likely to work on behalf of the newcomers, led to its replacement by the *Fundação Nacional do Índio* (National Indian Foundation) or FUNAI. However, the flood of incomers only increased as governments in search of economic growth encouraged the exploitation of the North, particularly after gold was discovered in the Amazon region. In the northern region of Roraima, the white population rose from 80,000 in the 1970s to 215,000 in 1991. The indigenous people, lacking immunity to diseases brought in by the settlers, were devastated, large numbers losing their lives to illness and malnutrition. Distrustful of the government agencies, they created their own political movement, the Council of Indigenous Peoples and

Organisations of Brazil. They described the government's attitude to them in the twentieth century as genocide and protested in 2000 at celebrations to mark the 500th anniversary of the discovery of Brazil.

Brazil is the biggest Catholic country in the world, but like the rest of South America, it has seen a rise in Protestantism. Evangelical or Pentecostal Protestantism has proved attractive to the poor who find the messages championing hard work, discipline and family life more relevant to their lives. More than 15 per cent of the population – around 20 million – are now Protestant.

Brazil at the end of the twentieth century still had its share of problems. Its internal inequality grated with the view of the country from the outside as the land of samba and carnival while the unfair distribution of wealth, discrimination, violent crime, rural poverty and urban blight weighed heavily on all who lived there.

The Miracle of Twenty-First Century Brazil

Described by US President Barack Obama in 2009 as 'the most popular politician on earth', Lula da Silva of the Workers' Party is undoubtedly one of the most successful politicians Brazil has ever produced. Before he finally won in 2002, however, he fought and lost the 1989, 1994 and 1998 presidential elections. In 2002, he won the presidency with more than 60 per cent of the national vote in the run-off. His opponent was José Serra (b.1942) of the Brazilian Social Democracy Party who gained 38.7 per cent.

President Lula had a background that was probably unlike any other leader of a major nation. He was born in Pernambuco in 1945, the seventh of eight children and moved to São Paulo with his family at the age of seven. When it transpired that his father already had a second family there, his mother moved with her children into a small room at the back of a bar. Lula did not learn to read until he was ten years old but had to leave school at twelve in order to earn money for his family, working as a shoeshine boy and a street vendor. By fourteen he was working a lathe in a factory that processed copper. In his late teens, he became active with the Workers' Union, eventually holding several important posts. In 1975 he was elected president of the Steel Workers' Union of São Bernardo do Campo and Diadema in the region of São Paolo that was home to much of Brazil's car-manufacturing industry. During military rule, he was active on behalf of the union, helping to organise several major strikes for which he was jailed for a month. He was a founding member of the Workers' Party and in 1983 helped found the *Central Única dos Trabalhadores* (CUT) union association. He won a seat in Congress in 1986, polling the most votes in the country and stood for president for the first time in 1989.

Lula's socialist politics initially gave rise to fears in the markets about his monetary policies and, indeed, inflation rose in the months following the election, the value of the *real* dropped and Brazil's credit rating was downgraded. Before long, to the disappointment of his leftist colleagues, he had convinced the money men that he was not going to radically change the policies of Cardoso's government and that the Brazilian Central Bank would persevere with the job of maintaining low inflation. It was a wise decision because the Brazilian economy experienced significant growth in the next few years. During his administration legislation was passed reforming tax, pensions, labour and the judiciary. Many of his former colleagues on the left were disappointed with his moderate approach and his alliances with former conservative presidents Sarney and Collor. Nonetheless, he was resoundingly elected for a second term in 2006, defeating Geraldo Alckmin (b.1952) of the PSDB in the run-off by 60.38 per cent to 39.17 per cent.

Lula made the eradication of hunger in Brazil a high priority with the campaign *Fome Zero* (Zero Hunger). Programmes were put in place to irrigate the semi-arid region of Sertão, to combat teenage pregnancy and to bolster family agricultural concerns, amongst other measures. Lula brought together a variety of social welfare programmes under the umbrella of *Bolsa Família* (Family Allowance) that rewarded families for the school attendance of their children and provided allowances for food and gas for cooking. At the start of his second term, he created the Growth Acceleration Programme, an investment programme with the aim of improving Brazil's infrastructure which would, as a result, stimulate the private sector and create jobs. In January 2008, Brazil became a net creditor for the first time, having for decades been the largest foreign debtor amongst emerging economies.

Lula helped to take Brazil's credibility as a world power to new levels and had the ambition to gain the country a permanent seat on the United Nations Security Council. He failed in this, but his pragmatism led to him becoming a mediator in many issues and disputes involving countries not just in the southern hemisphere but around the world. By the time he left office, his policies had significantly raised the living standards of the Brazilian people, the middle class rising from 37 per cent of the population to 50 per cent.

The Brazilian Constitution did not allow Lula to stand for a third term. The two main candidates were Dilma Rousseff (b.1947) of the Workers' Party, Lula's former Chief of Staff, and José Serra of the PSDB who had lost to Lula in 2002. It was anticipated that Rousseff would continue with the policies of her predecessor, maintaining and increasing partnerships with other developing nations and lobbying for the seat on the Security Council. Serra would naturally sever ties with Lula's left-wing allies in Latin America, such as Bolivia and Venezuela, endangering Brazilian investments in energy in those countries. Generally, however, it was thought that there was little to choose between these two main candidates in terms of the economy. Each would maintain a budget surplus in order to make public debt payments, reducing the ratio of debt to GDP.

Rousseff defeated Serra in the run-off by 56.05 per cent to 43.95 per cent to become the sixth Latin American woman elected as head of state.

Dilma Rousseff was from Belo Horizonte in Minas Gerais, born in 1947 to a Bulgarian lawyer and businessman and a schoolteacher. Her father had fled persecution of Communists in Bulgaria in 1929 and arrived in Brazil in the 1930s. Dilma Rousseff became active in socialist politics in 1967, as a member of *Política Operária* (Workers' Politics) or POLOP which was part of the Brazilian Socialist Party. Later she joined the far left *Comando de Libertação Nacional* (Command of National Liberation) or COLINA which favoured the use of arms in the struggle against military rule. COLINA merged with *Vanguarda Popular Revolucionária* (Popular Revolutionary Vanguard) to form *Vanguarda Armada Revolucionária Palmares* (Revolutionary Armed Vanguard Palmares), a body claiming to be a 'political-military organisation of Marxist Leninist partisan orientation which aims to fulfil the tasks of the revolutionary war and the establishment of the working class party, in order to seize power and build socialism'. Rousseff became one of the organisation's leaders, said to have led strikes and organised bank robberies, although she denies that she was more than an ordinary member. In 1970, this 'Joan of Arc' of the guerrilla movement, as the prosecutor described her, was arrested. She was sentenced to six years in prison but was released after three. Her political rights were suspended for eighteen years. Throwing herself into legitimate politics after the end of military rule, she became Municipal Secretary of the Treasury in Porto Alegre and then Secretary of Energy for Rio Grande do Sul. After he was elected president, Lula appointed her Minister of Energy and then, in 2005, his Chief of Staff. She took office as president on 1 January 2011, promising to continue her predecessor's fight against poverty in Brazil and to maintain the economic growth the country had been experiencing.

During Lula's administration, Brazil had been granted the right to stage not only the 2014 FIFA World Cup, but Rio de Janeiro was given the 2016 Olympic Games. It was a recognition of how far Brazil had come in the preceding decade and an opportunity to place the country firmly in the world's gaze. Infrastructure projects had to be launched in the twelve cities hosting World Cup matches and in Rio where the Olympics would take place. The background to these challenges, however, was the ongoing economic crisis in Europe and the United States and President Rousseff had to take cautionary measures to protect the Brazilian economy when she came to office. These helped to reduce growth in GDP.

Around 16 million Brazilians remain in absolute poverty and Rousseff took steps to alleviate this with the announcement of the programme *Brasil Sem Miséria* (Brazil Without Poverty). Despite criticism, however, as the economy stuttered during her first three years in office she retained the highest approval rating of any president since military rule. This changed in summer of 2013, as the world's media descended on the country for the FIFA Confederations Cup, the football tournament staged in the host country the summer before the World Cup. Protests erupted in several Brazilian cities against increases in the prices of bus, train and metro tickets. Initially organised by *Movimento Passe Livre* (Free Fare Movement), the protests grew to include other issues such as police brutality, social service provision and the vast sums of money being spent on the two sporting events. It was the largest protest since the 1992 demonstrations against the government of President Collor and came to be known as the Salad Uprising, the 'V for Vinegar' Movement – after a journalist was arrested for possession of vinegar which eases the effects of tear gas – or the Brazilian Spring.

In response to the riots, President Rousseff pledged to spend 50 million *reals* (£13.5 million) on improvements to public transport. Other concessions were made, such as petroleum monies being directed at educational provision, a National Pact to improve education, health and public transport and the revocation of the 'Gay Cure' Bill that authorised sexual orientation therapy for lesbian, gay and bisexual people.

Since 2003, nearly 40 million Brazilians have been lifted out of poverty. A nation where a few decades earlier, protest was being suppressed by violence and many were unable to feed their families was now on the crest of a consumer wave and the new members of the middle class were choosing what make of car or television to purchase. This boom itself engendered a growth rate in GDP of 7.5 per cent by 2010, Brazil's best economic performance in twenty-five years. In 2012, it overtook the United Kingdom to become the world's sixth-largest economy. This phenomenal growth is partly due to its relationship with China, now Brazil's largest trading partner and its membership of BRIC, a trading group consisting of countries experiencing extraordinary economic development – Brazil, Russia, India and China. It is a group that symbolises the shift in power away from the traditionally powerful countries of the G7 (USA, UK, France, Italy, Germany, Canada and Japan) towards these nations of the developing world. It is suggested by some that the combined economies of the BRIC countries could overtake those of the G7 by 2027. Whatever actually transpires, it is evident that Brazil's economy will become less dependent on its American connections but increasingly dependent on both its regional ties and its partners in the BRICS (South Africa joined in 2010) trading bloc.

In recent times, agriculture has greatly contributed to Brazil's economic development. In the first quarter of 2013, it increased production by 9.7 per cent and a further 3.9 per cent in the second quarter. This was mainly derived from massive increases in soy production with Brazil the second-largest producer in the world of soybeans after the United States. In the last 35 years soy production has grown by 3000 per cent, with soybean and soybean derivatives earning Brazil more than US$9 billion a year.

The economy has slowed in the past year, however, expanding by less than 2 per cent, a fall put into sharp focus by the decade of dramatic growth it has experienced.

Changes in agriculture and land use are creating problems, of course. Deforestation, loss of biodiversity and water pollution have been the consequences of cattle rearing and soy production in the Amazônia Legal and Cerrado grassland regions. Seventy-four million cattle graze in the former area and almost half of the latter (386,000 square miles) have been burned and cleared for cattle pasture or have been planted with soybeans, corn and sugarcane. The soy and corn are important ingredients of cattle feed and the sugarcane is used in the production of ethanol. More than any other country, Brazil relies on ethanol as an ingredient of fuel for motor vehicles.

More than 231,000 square miles of Amazonian rainforest have been destroyed since 1970, a huge amount of it between 2000 and 2010, mostly in response to a global demand for wood and soybeans. This is a major source of pollution, biodiversity loss and greenhouse gas emissions, not just in Brazil, but around the world. It has been announced by the Brazilian Ministry of the Environment that there has been a decrease since the middle of 2011 as the Brazilian government promotes sustainability and monitors deforestation using satellites and monitoring programmes. It claims that it will also reduce deforestation by closing down illegal sawmills and impounding illegal timber and vehicles transporting it. Deforestation and illegal logging remain very serious issues, however.

Environmental issues are, of course, of major interest to both Brazil and the rest of the world. Efforts have been made to deal with the impact of agriculture and industrialisation on the country. The use of ethanol is one sign that the Brazilian government has taken heed of global concerns as is the fact that Brazil is now home to two sustainable cities – Porto Alegre and Curitiba. Nonetheless, major concerns remain which threaten the fantastically diverse flora and fauna of Brazil.

*

With growth and foreign investment slowing recently, the stock market falling and the *real* losing value against the dollar, after a decade of remarkable success, it seems that challenges may lie ahead for the Brazilian economy. Our view of Brazil will depend on how it deals with not only that, however. To truly become a respected and admired global power, the fight to eradicate poverty in Brazil must continue, the gap between rich and poor must be reduced and the social issues brought to global attention by the Brazilian Spring must be dealt with. Only then will the land of samba, carnival and the 'beautiful game', in the words of President Juscelino Kubitschek, 'come of age'.

Suggested Further Reading

Burns, E Bradford, *A Documentary History of Brazil*. New York: Alfred A. Knopf, 3rd edition, 1993

Faust, Boris, *A Concise History of Brazil*. New York: Cambridge University Press, 1999

Levine, Robert M, *The History of Brazil*. New York: Palgrave Macmillan, 2003

Skidmore, Thomas E, *Brazil: Five Centuries of Change*. New York: Oxford University Press, 2nd edition, 2009

Smith, Dr Joseph, *A History of Brazil*. London: Longman, 2002

Index

Index

Index